On Social Marketing and Social Change

Selected Readings 2005-2009

R. Craig Lefebvre PhD

ISBN: 1449561934
ISBN-13: 9781449561932

On Social Marketing and Social Change: The Back Story

On 4 March 2005 I stepped into the new world of social media. I had been reading and hearing about blogs, podcasts and online social networks, and decided it was worth a look. It also seemed like a good way for me to write down some of my thoughts and experiences without the hassle and aggravation of creating articles for peer review publications. If nothing else, my blog would be my professional diary: creating accounts that, if nothing else, I could refer back to later rather than resorting to leafing through old notebooks and notepads. Who knows, maybe some body else will read them as well and we can talk about them?

I started out on radio-blogs (where the posts still exist) as 'R. Craig Lefebvre's Social Marketing Blog.' Even then, getting my name and the social marketing topic to be found by search engines was one of the early pieces of advice I gleaned from other blogs and the one or two books on blogging then available.

I started off: "This site focuses on news and commentary about the use of marketing concepts and techniques to influence the behavior of segments of the population. "Social" implies that the outcomes are ones that will benefit the individual and society-at-large, though as we will see, many times marketing is used for less altruistic and transparent purposes as well. These enterprises will also be fair game." My second post that same day was about the overlooked importance of 'Place' in the marketing mix: "think of Place not just as a distribution channel for messages and their related products…but as a location where people can try or engage in the target behavior (in marketing terms, where they can 'buy' the product). After all, that's what we are marketing - not the pamphlet or PSA."[1]

By the next day, 'Social marketing in the news (or can a one-armed gangly googler add value)' appeared as a regular weekly update and continued for several years until my Google alerts were swamped by the new use of 'social marketing' to refer to marketing in social media channels, particularly social network sites. Many social marketers today bristle at the idea of 'their' term being stolen by the heathens; having watched it unfold, it was more a story of dereliction than stealth.

By January 2006 I knew I had outgrown what Radio Userland was offering, and moved the blog to Typepad and renamed it 'On Social Marketing and Social

Change' where it is today.[2] As I write this, there are now over 800 posts available there.

My exploration of blogging has taken me deeply into the social marketing space, but more importantly, it opened up unforeseen opportunities to become involved in social and mobile media. This book is another format to introduce and reacquaint some of you with this journey. I have not tried to do this in chronological order as the journey has been anything but linear. And given the inability of print to embed the numerous links that demonstrate the interconnectedness of many of the posts, I have put them together into thematic categories like you would find them on the site. What I have done in putting this book together is to refer to my web analytics and selected from the most popular pages for many of these posts. And yes, there are a few that I believe you should read even if they didn't win the popularity contest.

Section I, *On Social Marketing* contains posts that are an orientation to my concept of what social marketing is and what it could be. To this latter point, I selected 'The Social Marketing Manifesto" to kick things off, even though it appeared later than some of the others. Without listing them all, beginning with "Making Change Happen" comes a collection of ideas about social marketing. Later I cover some ideas from outside the field that are important for us to incorporate into our thinking about social change including the Total Market Approach, the Base of the Pyramid idea, and Creative Capitalism. And 'No!' these approaches are not just for people practicing in the 'developing world' – all nations are developing.

People Formerly Known as the Audience introduces the soul of social marketing: people. If there is a theme to this collection, it is that social marketers need to stop thinking about passive audiences, or persons they invite to focus groups, and seek to understand them and know them as people first who have as much to contribute to what we do as the so-called experts.

A battle cry of mine for over a dozen years has been on the tyranny of focus groups and the irrational belief that these contrived and sterile environments are somehow giving us wisdom about people we serve. *Into the Jungle* is a series of posts about attitude as much as it is about methods, and explores some of the characteristics of people we use to call 'audiences.' Some of the groups that come into focus include people with low literacy skills, the people who make policy, the people who heal and care for sick children and their families and those who have adopted the new media.

In *The Marketing Blender* are a number of riffs I have done on the 4Ps of product, price, place and promotion. An intention of many of these articles, beginning with 'Health communication; The 5% solution,' is to challenge readers to examine their default behavior of using communication to solve the problems they are presented. Ideas about demarketing, price, and place-based interventions are covered as options, particularly in the context of obesity prevention.

Bring on Social Media is a section that many regular readers of the blog would have been surprised to not see here, though there are some social marketers who will wonder what all of it has to do with social marketing ('aren't those the people trying to steal our words?!'). In a few words here's my point-of-view (POV): when the research informs us that interpersonal communication is the most powerful behavior change modality, we have a responsibility to harness that for social good and to scale up interventions. Social media and mobile technologies, I believe, are the most effective ways we yet have to move the personal-to-one to the personal-with-many. Think about it...

One person you will see missing in virtually every text on social marketing is the manager. Many of us get caught up in teaching the doing, but having been a manager of many simpler but usually quite complex social marketing programs, I realize that managing the doing is, in the longer term, the more sustainable model for social marketing practice. So managers, and aspiring ones, the section *A Manager's POV* is for you. In it I spend as much time looking at marketing management practice in the private sector and try to make it relevant to the public and nonprofit (NGO) sectors as well (see 'McDonald's Secrets of Success' and 'Learn from P&G' in particular). I also hope that some of you will find the discussions of coalitions and partnerships, as well as fear, world-changing.

Over the past two years, I have been getting more involved in the area of design thinking, and sometimes those experiences have seeped into the blog (not as much as it should, but stay tuned on the blog). Design thinking starts where social marketing does, or should – with people. The collection of posts in *Design Thinking* are the beginning of the explorations of overlap and cross-fertilization across these two areas.

The final section, *The Change We Need* includes the advocacy pieces for how social marketing should be participating in the social change space, another arena where we have been underrepresented and risk becoming inconsequential. I was delighted that one of them, 'The Change We Need: New Ways of Thinking About Social Issues," was reproduced in Social Marketing Quarterly.[3] Perhaps, these posts will inspire you to lift the conversation about social marketing from 4Ps and formative research to change. As several of my blogging friends have commented in the past: when will you guys stop talking about it and start doing it? When indeed.

Before leaving the back story, I want to acknowledge the known and unknown heroes that have been my models, mentors, colleagues and friends in this social media space (so far). From the early days, Steve Rubin at MicroPersuasion, Rohit Bhargava at Influential Marketing Blog, Paul Revere at The Pump Handle (the only other public health blog when I started), Katya Andresen at her Non-Profit Marketing Blog, Marc van Gurp at Houtlust (now Osocio), Grant Mc-Cracken at This Blog Sits at the Intersection of Anthropology and Economics, danah boyd at Zephoria, Nancy Schwartz at Getting Attention, and the folks at Futurelab's Blog, were among a group of bloggers I read, linked to and emulated regularly. Since my blog appeared, I have been followed into the social media space by a number of other social marketers including Nedra Weinreich at Spare Change (who did her first post as a guest blogger with me), Alexandra Bornkessel at SocialButterfly, Michael Newton-Ward at Social Marketing Panorama, and Andre Blackman of Pulse + Signal whose company and collegiality extend beyond the virtual spaces we co-occupy. There have been many other bloggers, teachers and researchers over the years, and the list could go on...social media does tend to lead to expansive social networks! But for now I will stop here; perhaps there will be another opportunity to pick up where I left off.

So read slow, think long and rock on! The world is counting on us.

Notes
1. http://radio-weblogs.com/0144797/2005/03/04.html
2. http://socialmarketing.blogs.com
3. Lefebvre, RC. The change we need: New ways of thinking about social issues. *Social Marketing Quarterly* 2009;**15**:142-144

Marketing for Social Improvement

A Social Marketing Manifesto

Over the past decade or more, <u>social marketing has been put into a straitjacket</u>. I can't put a firm date on it, but I remember becoming concerned in the early 1990s that the *tyranny of focus groups* had taken over how market research 'should' be conducted because that's what the Office of Management and Budget (OMB) would allow Federal agencies to do without extensive and prolonged bureaucratic reviews of research protocols (psst: now it's *ethnographic research*). Then there was the unexamined adoption by many people (some who should have known better) of the transtheoretical (aka stages of change) model of behavior change as 'our theory' - as it was recently referred to on the social marketing list serve - when it's least well-suited for guiding social or population change efforts. In other circles, social marketing became equated with the distribution and promotion of subsidized commodities - and sales targets reigned supreme. And the mantra of behavior change as the goal of social marketing got twisted from its original call as a population-based methodology to one focused exclusively on individuals - until some of those proponents finally figured out that it is a bigger world than *pros and cons* and *blaming the victim* isn't just a slogan.

<u>What has been lost in all of this is the soul of social marketing and its subsequent arrested development</u>. Reductionist paradigms supported a model of rational choice where pros and cons were all that were needed to change behavior in 'contemplative' audiences through some sort of convoluted 'exchange relationship.'

People were to change through social marketing programs to 'improve society;' that the community or society may be the issue apparently never occurred to some people. <u>That communities could be the context of change, and even the drivers of change, was rarely acknowledged - even though some of the pioneers of this field developed and applied the social marketing model in community settings.</u> And process measures, or outputs, such as the number of people reached with a public service campaign, the number of brochures distributed or the number of condoms sold became the means to justify the ends of the programs - not health behavior change or health impact.

That won't change in one post, but it starts here for me. <u>It's time for a manifesto for social marketing; not one aimed at the 'outside' world, but one aimed at the insiders.</u> By insiders I'm not referring just to the people and organizations associated with social marketing, but the ones standing on the edges, humming the tunes, sipping the Kool-Aid but too cool to dance: the government agencies, foundations, health departments, schools of public health, NGOs and voluntary organizations that define social marketing to fit their version of reality. That find it too applied, too 'socialistic' (that 'social' word), too expensive or too... scary because it challenges too many of their core beliefs and challenges them to act, not describe and analyze. Then there are the agencies and individuals who are simply confused by the whole thing because so many different definitions of what is social marketing are out there. Inevitably there are a few who don't want to expend the cognitive effort it takes to be deliberate, systematic and strategic in their thinking and planning (my *Nike planners* - they just do it).

I made a comment on Monday at the Conversations session that has come back to me several times in 24 hours: *in reviewing at least four new texts on social marketing over the past year or so, I haven't seen a total of 4 new ideas among them.* **The field has become an echo chamber.** No wonder people question its relevance in this day and age! The old models of social marketing are becoming fossils. Here are six things I believe are important for a new social marketing.

Focusing on audiences.   Understanding and emphasizing with their wants and needs, aspirations, lifestyle, freedom of choice. And not just those audiences identified by our epidemiological friends as having the greatest need, or by our public relations colleagues as the low hanging fruit, but the people who are crucial to the success of our programs - the volunteers, business leaders, distributors, partner organizations, media representatives and policy makers to name a few.

Targeting aggregated behavior change. Priority segments of the population, not individuals, are the focus of programs. Social marketing must be based on theoretical models that guide the selection of the most relevant determinants, priority audiences, objectives, interventions and evaluations for population-based behavior change such as theories of diffusion of innovations, social networks, community assets, political economics and social capital. My belief is that the major reason we cannot achieve public health impact for many of our interventions like HIV prevention is that we do not design interventions for scale, we design them with models of behavior change that are most effective with individuals.

Designing behaviors that fit their reality. We need to bring to behavior change the same insight, thought and rigor that designers bring to their work in developing products, services and experiences. If more social marketers thought like designers, and didn't act as technicians plugging the latest scientific finding into their 'message machine or wheel' my hunch is we'd be more successful - and sleep better. Behaviors, not just messages, need to be tailored for people's real lives - not the one we imagine or theorize they have, if we think about them at all.

Rebalancing incentives and costs for maintaining or changing behaviors. Though you might say 'gotcha! - back to pros and cons,' it's a bigger idea than that. Rebalancing doesn't mean convincing a person to use a new set of weights in their personal equation to calculate risks and benefits of acting in certain ways. People LEARN new behaviors and what I am mystified by is how complex theories are dragged out to explain and try to modify behaviors when simple learning principles like what gets associated with what and what gets rewarded and punished (or not) are often the elegantly simple solution. Rebalancing also means adjusting the environment, policies and marketplace whenever possible to shift power to the individual to have freedom to choose and enjoy basic human rights. We need to start asking ourselves questions like: where do inequities in health status stem from? Is income generation a prerequisite for health improvement in impoverished communities? How do we allow markets to work for the poor and vulnerable?

Creating opportunities and access to try, practice and sustain behaviors. We must take distribution systems, in all their forms and expressions, as seriously - if not more so - as the messages and creative products we produce. People do not think or choose their way to new behaviors - they must have access to the information they need to make informed choices (in ways, places and times that literacy, cultural and other considerations should inherently inform: relevance should never be an after thought in social marketing). And they must have the opportunities to try new behaviors, practice them and then be able to sustain them. Behavior change is not a one-off proposition.

Communicating these behaviors, incentives and opportunities to priority audiences and letting people experience them. ALL social marketing programs are mired in the last century when it comes to models of communication. The reflexive urge to continue with top down, command and control techniques will continue for awhile (aka Source - Message - Channel - Receiver or inoculation models). However, as regular readers of this blog may have discerned, I hold out that the technological revolutions we are experiencing in communications will lead to the adoption of modern communication models to frame our thinking and activities - even if many have to change while kicking and screaming or longing for 'the good ol' days.' And then there are the questions we started asking 5 years ago about <u>how do we apply what we know about positioning and brands to develop powerful and sustained behavior change programs, and not just logos and tag lines</u> or ... mission statements.

I yield the floor...

Making Change Happen:
The Social Marketing Approach

Achieving success in improving people's health, positively influencing social conditions, enabling people to lift themselves out of poverty and achieving social justice and equity are some of the focus points of social marketing. Since its original formulation, countless people and organizations in the world have observed, experimented and, more importantly, applied the ideas of marketing to social issues. Their work, though poorly chronicled in the professional literature (and a weakness hindering its broader acceptance in professional communities), has been documented and put into systematic form in several major publications and books on the subject. There are also several cookbooks for practitioners to help them apply social marketing.

For the past year, I have been using variations of this graphic in presentations to visually display in one place the essential elements of social marketing. It is designed for posting on your wall, serving as your screen saver, going anywhere with you so you can quickly access the major ingredients as you engage in program design. It's not a textbook to wade through, a cookbook to leaf through, or a workbook to apply to each program you design. Rather, *it is a map — not focused on the topology of your specific problem, not highlighting the shortest or even best route to a solution, but a reminder of the space you are in as you attempt to make change happen among people in need, organizations that serve them and community leaders and policymakers who create the opportunities and allocate the resources to support these efforts.* The idea is to begin at the center and then work your way out to the edges where the program elements (tactics) take shape.

What the graphic depicts is an expansion of the essential components of social marketing as I currently distill them from the research and being involved in the development of hundreds of programs and campaigns. Take a look and then I'll briefly discuss the pieces.

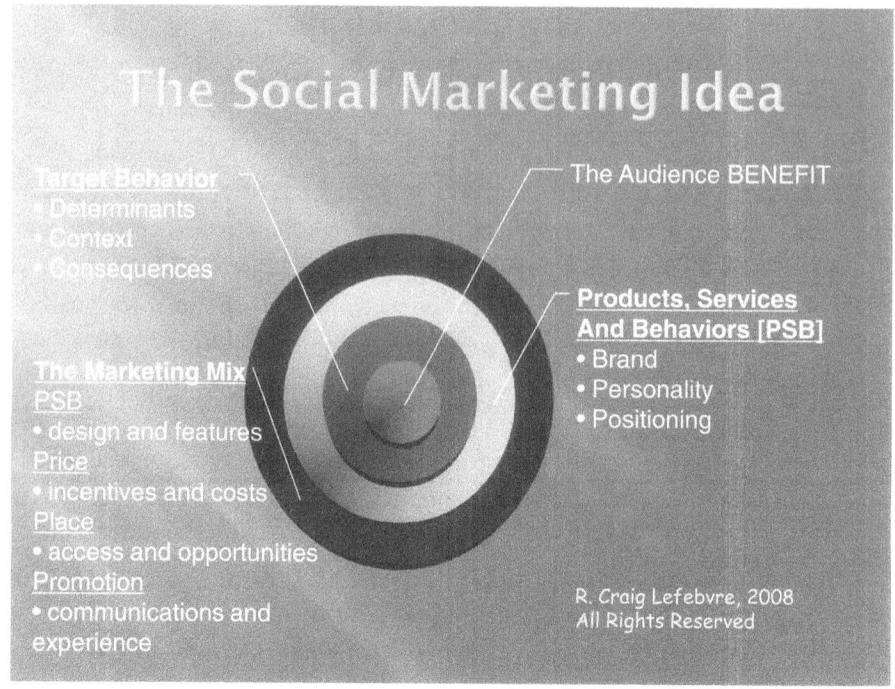

THE SOCIAL MARKETIG IDEA

The social marketing idea consists of 4 bands that exist for each priority audience or market a program addresses. These bands are the 4 big ideas in social marketing.

They are what distinguish social marketing from strictly communication, community-based methods, education, economic and advocacy efforts aimed at social change.

The Audience Benefit

Benefits exist in the mind of the audience, consumer or user. They are not tangible things, though tangible items can sometimes capture the essence of a benefit if carefully designed. Benefits tap into the underlying motivations of groups of people (or segments); they are not health, a cleaner environment, access to services or even money. For example, in our work with state children's health insurance programs, the audience insight into the benefit for parents to enroll in SCHIPs [State Childrens' Health Insurance Programs] was not access to care; it was peace-of-mind. It was being able to allow their child to fully participate in life like other kids without the parent's nagging concern about 'what happens if...?" Likewise, a major barrier to these same parents enrolling in the program was, strangely enough, the concern that by their enrolling in the program they were taking the spot of someone who they believed would be more in need of it than them. I say 'strangely' because the program administrators had not even conceived of that possibility.

Once you experience the power of listening to an audience for the benefit, rather than having the experts or policymakers dictate it, the results can be world changing.

Target Behavior

The influence of social marketing in public health circles was its focus on population-based behavior change – not increasing awareness, changing attitudes or influencing perceptions and intentions as most health campaigns did then (and even to some extent now). Squarely placing behavior change as the outcome of interest has enormous implications for program architecture and design; it also makes results and accountability more observable too.

Under the target behavior, there are 3 sets of questions program designers must address – the nature of those questions will vary depending on the theoretical or ideological perspective they bring to the task. What the social marketing approach embraces is to understand the determinants, context and consequences of current behaviors, and desired ones, from the point-of-view (POV) of the audience. The determinants can include any number of variables specified by behavioral theory and research. However, the perspective on determinants needs to broaden beyond individual ones to include the many social determinants as well, some of which may fall under the rubric of context. Context is the 'ground' in the gestalt sense of the word in which individual behaviors 'figure' against the social and physical 'ground' in which people live. Poverty, housing conditions, social capital, the quality of built and natural environments, working conditions and public policies are examples of context – a context not just to understand, but also to potentially target for change in order to bring about healthier conditions and behaviors.

Finally, the consequences of current and alternative behaviors need to be assessed - see applied behavior analysis[1]. What intrinsic, social and other rewards, modulators and punishments exist or can be created to enable people to move to healthier and more productive lives? Economists point to monetary rewards and penalties as one of the more important policy levers in influencing behavior change[2]. Money has the property of being whatever people want it to be (in terms of how they think about it and exchange it for favored goods and services). Yet, in daily life there are countless other sources of rewards and punishments (or at least inhibitors) for current behaviors and healthier alternatives that marketers concern themselves with in this analysis.

Products, Services and Behaviors

One of the great dividing lines between social marketing practitioners in the developing world and the developed world has been erased. That is between social marketing that focuses on product sales and the movement of commodities and social marketing that focuses on behavior change. What has become clear to both 'camps' is that products and services can be necessary, but not sufficient, conditions to improve health (e.g., condoms for HIV prevention, LLINs - long-lasting insecticide-treated nets, for malaria control). What's crucial, and the point that the advocates of free distribution leave out and is the rallying point for all social marketers, is that people must use these products and services (e.g., family planning, testing and counseling centers, prenatal clinics) and change behaviors to impact morbidity and mortality. These are the most important things to be measuring and influencing. We are not satisfied with sales figures, visits, products distributed, exposure and other measures of process - behavioral outcomes define success. Health and social outcomes then follow.

The point that gets lost on the behavior change proponents is that behavior change is an incremental process that must start with people's current realities and that the suggested behaviors must be relevant to their lives – not a theory or research finding. Thus, while programs may have desired behavioral outcomes, helping people get to that point may mean designing programs that focus on shaping, or targeting incremental, behaviors. For example, while consistent use of a condom in high risk situations may be an objective for an HIV prevention program, depending on the audience the incremental behavioral steps might include seeking out and getting one, negotiating with a partner to use it and correctly using it. When thinking about HIV prevention more broadly, other behavioral steps include getting tested for HIV, being faithful to a partner, abstaining from sex and getting prophylactic treatment if pregnant and HIV positive to prevent HIV transmission to the infant. The important point that social marketing brings to this discussion is that <u>the behaviors we focus on should be ones that the people we work with agree are relevant, possible and they believe they are able to do in their daily lives (not just as part of a research protocol)</u>. If not, then we need to back up and work on earlier steps in the behavior change (or behavior chain) process.

Whether it is a behavior in the chain of behavioral steps to the ultimate target behavior, or a product or service offering that supports or enables behavior change, the ideas of branding, personality (image or tone) and positioning come into strategic play. Explicit here is the need to understand the competition, whether it is other organizations, interests and programs or competing behaviors (doing one thing versus another). Branding is not the logo, theme song and tagline of a campaign or a program. It is what the behavior and program mean to the people. An exemplar of this approach is in developing conservation programs in tropical developing countries, where Rare's programs[3] use a threatened species for image and communication purposes, but the brand is Pride that supports behavior and conservation objectives. It's unusual to find such sophisticated use of brands in social marketing programs (truth is another good example[4]) because most programs forget that they are in the psychology business, not dictation.

The Marketing Mix

What we need to be better at in social marketing is understanding that <u>our products, services and behaviors have to be designed with specific features that appeal to our target audience</u>. The 5 A Day program, for instance, designed behaviors to support the objective of increasing the number of servings of fruits and vegetables people eat each day by listening to and then incorporating the ideas of the priority audience – behaviors that focused on ease and convenience - rather than developing and promoting recipes (as a counter example) that had more fruits and vegetables in them. <u>Our products and services likewise need to be thought about from a design POV[5] – how their use and the experiences they create for the audience reinforce or inhibit healthier choices and facilitate or impede access and opportunities to engage with them.</u>

Social marketing has taken the idea of price beyond monetary ones to include psychological, social, geographic and other rewards and punishments for everyday behaviors. <u>An exclusive focus on just monetary costs limits social marketing</u>

programs and leads to marketing myopia just as much as a focus on psychological, social or physical barriers does. If we understand the consequences of
behavior and behavior change, then we can begin to judge the salience of various
levels and types of prices for current and alternative behaviors from the audience POV. We then have the chance to develop programs that realign incentives
and costs for products, services and behaviors that resonate with the market and
lead to better outcomes.

Access and opportunities to healthier and health-promoting products, services
and behaviors is the big step between wanting to engage in a healthier lifestyle
and being able to do it (placing opportunity within an arm's reach of desire).
Access to products and services, in concept, is fairly straightforward – though
execution and logistics in resource poor environments to make these a reality can
be daunting. Equally important, especially to the behavior change minded social
marketer, is creating access and opportunities to perform the healthier alternatives – or not practice the unhealthier ones. Clean indoor air laws clearly address
the latter issue, while increasing the availability of fresh fruits and vegetables,
having more safe places to be physically active and offering healthier options in
restaurants and fast service establishments are examples of improving access and
opportunities to engage in healthy behaviors.

The promotion of a target behavior is the realm of persuasive communications efforts. While much attention is given by many practitioners and people
who should know better as to how to craft messages and identify channels, select credible sources, and target messages to receivers of wisdom, the S-C-M-R
model is under deservedly heavy fire by theory, evidence and new technologies
that are reconceptualizing the role of the audience as a producer and not just
a passive recipient of health information (See: *The Audience as Producer*). In social
marketing, our aim needs to be higher. An under-appreciated aspect of communication theory that supports marketing, and especially the creation of markets,
is agenda-setting theory[7]: how to develop and marshal support for public policy
initiatives among policymakers, the media, opinion leaders and the general public. Media advocacy and social marketing, while favoring different tactics, both
focus (or should) on broader population change objectives that alter the 4P
context in which behavior occurs. It's no accident that many tobacco control
policy initiatives focus on increasing the price of tobacco, restricting access
and sales, removing opportunities to smoke, banning various promotions
and advertising activities, and increasing access and opportunities for smoking

cessation services. Too few social marketing efforts expand beyond IP marketing efforts that favor communication tactics and vehicles – the traditional "un-4Ps of PSAs, posters, pamphlets and publicity" that now include entertainment, social and mobile media. <u>Promotions (communications) need to work with the other 3Ps in an integrated way to increase the likelihood that a high percentage of people in our priority audience engage in healthier and socially beneficial behaviors.</u>

A picture, and about 2,000 words, of what I see as **the social marketing idea**. I invite you to provide your own takeaway.

Notes
1. http://en.wikipedia.org/wiki/Applied_behavior_analysis
2. http://www.who.int/heli/economics/econinstruments/en/index.html
3. http://www.ssireview.org/articles/entry/the_cultural_touch/
4. http://www.protectthetruth.org/truthcampaign.htm
5. http://metacool.typepad.com/metacool/2006/08/so_we_must_cons.html
6. Lefebvre, R.C., Doner, L., Johnston, C., Loughrey, K., Balch, G., Sutton, S.M. Use of database marketing and consumer-based health communication in message design: An example from the Office of Cancer Communications' "5 a Day for Better Health" program. In: Maibach E, Parrott R, eds. *Designing Health Messages: Approaches from Communication Theory and Public Health Practice.* Newburg Park, California: Sage Publications, 1995:217–46.
7. http://en.wikipedia.org/wiki/Agenda_setting

Health Communications, Social Marketing and Coke

Recent graduates of health communications and public health programs like to ask me what the differences are between health communications and social marketing. Today, one of these students carefully pointed out that social marketing is the 'backbone' of health communications because it leads communicators to segment their audience, understand them (conduct research) and then focus on behavior change. "All of those things are true," I said, "for any good health communication program."

What the students, and apparently others who are having these debates in classrooms and staff meetings, miss is the marketing mix. As I described my take on the differences with a Coke analogy, they became clear (or so she said anyway). Here it is for you to try on (with apologies to Coke and their agencies).

Health communicators are like the advertising agencies for Coke. Their job is to understand the audience, create engaging and persuasive communication and deliver it in ways that raise awareness of the brand and maybe even increase purchase behaviors. If a person sees a Coke ad and is thirsty, but can't get to a store to buy one, finds no Cokes on the shelves when they get there, sees Pepsis are cheaper and/or really wants a diet Coke - no amount of advertising is going to fix those problems. And no advertising agency would dream of trying to do that.

Social marketers are like the marketing department for Coke. They need to be sure that the product line (behavioral choices) has in it something for every one - not one thing for everyone. They then focus on the distribution system so that anywhere someone is thirsty, a Coke is within an arm's reach of desire [and is why the recent vending machine agreement[1] was a victory for the beverage industry]. Now they focus on the pricing side of the equation, not only deciding what price a thirsty consumer will pay for a Coke, but how much to charge for it relative to the other beverage marketers - not just the other colas, when to have sales, send coupons to people, run contests and in other ways create incentives for people to buy Cokes.

And only then do they worry about jingles, furry polar bears in ads and public relations activities.

A big difference that demonstrates itself in so many meetings when as soon as the brainstorming begins, it's all about the 4Ps of posters, pamphlets, PSAs and publicity and not the 4Ps of marketing.

Note
1. http://www.usatoday.com/news/health/2006-05-03-soda-schools_x. htm

When is it Social Marketing?

A simple enough question that gets awfully complex when looking for it in case studies and other descriptions of practice (see BC Walks[1] and the many programs in *Social Marketing in the News* on the blog). Another article from this month's issue of *Preventing Chronic Disease* came up on my 'social marketing' RSS feed from PubMed and reading through it caused me to ask the question again. My concern with Cherokee Choices[2] isn't with the program they present. It's not even with their labeling of a seven-part cable television series of interviews with people who have experience with diabetes and three 30-second TV spots as a "Social Marketing Initiative."

It's that a publication and set of peer reviewers who want the statistical software [SPSS 13.0 (SPSS Inc, Chicago, Ill) and SPSS 12.0 (SPSS Inc, Chicago, Ill)], qualitative data analytic package [Atlas.ti (Atlas.ti Scientific Software Development GmbH, Berlin, Germany)] and body-fat analyzer [Futrex–6100XL body-fat analyzer (Spencer Medical Inc, Rancho Santa Margarita, Calif), which can measure between 3% and 45% of body fat] documented in the paper cannot suggest to the authors that a term like Health Communication, Mass Media or Television "Initiative" might be a more appropriate description of that component of the program.

Of course, it is all a matter of priorities I suppose. My suggestion is that the journal and its reviewers have a set of questions they can ask themselves when reviewing manuscripts that contain the term 'social marketing.'

1. Do the authors understand and have an insight into their target audience?
2. Are they focusing on behavior as their product (what are they encouraging a large number of people to adopt or sustain)?
3. Do they influence or try to alter the relative balance of incentives and costs for either maintaining the current behavior or adopting a new one?
4. Do they attempt to increase access and opportunities for the audience to try the new behavior and then sustain it?
5. Are communication and other promotional techniques used to assure that they reach and engage the audience in ways that are relevant, attention-getting, tap into existing motivations and aspirations and have sufficient frequency to be remembered and acted on?

If you can answer 'yes' to all of these questions, you may have a social marketing program. I say 'may' because you can meet these criteria with a diverse set of tactics that have no integrative strategy or focus for each audience. HOW the planners address each of these questions with their program is up to their own frame of reference, results of audience research, community participation, theoretical bent, review of evidence-based practices, morals, values, ego, etc.…. And how they obtain and analyze the data are another set of questions.

I believe that a lot of times it is not that people are confused about what is social marketing, they just need some help seeing it. Reviewers and editors can serve that function. Hope these questions are helpful.

Notes
1. http://www.ncbi.nlm.nih.gov/pubmed/16776891?dopt=Abstract
2. http://www.cdc.gov/PCD/issues/2006/jul/05_0221.htm

Critique and Models of Social Marketing

Two weeks ago Lisa Mighton posted on the social marketing list serve 'Criticism of Social Marketing.' With her permission, an edited version:

Recently I had some email exchanges with a colleague who works in development communication. This person finds that people are often critical of social marketing, particularly because of how it has been used for HIV/AIDS campaigning - eg., promoting condoms but not addressing the underlying reasons why people weren't using them. In what ways is this true; in what ways isn't it?

Here is my response:

How one uses social marketing is contingent on the implicit or explicit theory one has to explain and predict (and thus possibly influence) behavior. The use of an exchange model for social marketing programs, especially in the developing world where many social marketing programs involve the promotion of products (e.g., condoms, birth control methods, oral rehydration solutions and mosquito nets) that are made available through various nonprofit and for-profit distribution networks with prices typically well below competitors' offerings (due to subsidization by donor agencies), reflects an economic theory of man [Economic Man[1]] that emphasizes self-interest and rational decision-making. Though this position is tenable in the consumer and, to some extent, services marketing sector, the ascendance of behavioral economics[2] is due to the fact that this model has its shortcomings in other settings.

In the US and many other 'developed countries,' my perspective is that social marketing has grown out of efforts to apply behavioral theories such as social cognitive theory, the health belief model, the transtheoretical model (stages of change), diffusion theory and other psychological, social, community and political theories to population-based behavior change. As a consequence, there is much less emphasis on tangible products. Indeed, some of the earliest concerns of social marketers[3] centered around the notion of 'making the intangible tangible' – a concern, I'll point out, that exists to this day in the over reliance on developing communication products – whether they be posters, pamphlets, PSAs and publicity events (the 4Ps of not marketing, but communicating).

To your question, yes I would commiserate with your friend that many very real determinants of behavior are overlooked by, in my mind, a simplistic assumption that economic theories can be used for understanding, predicting and changing complex behaviors. When we first convened a group of 'domestic' and 'international' social marketers at an early Innovations in Social Marketing Conference, one inescapable conclusion several of us from both perspectives shared was that we truly came from different 'cultures,' tribes or traditions of social marketing. Rather than placing a value judgment on the differences, the question for world changing becomes: When do the different models make the most sense to apply to a specific health or social problem and in what circumstances?

Your friend is also not alone in their assessment of social marketing. It is a position that is even more vociferously voiced by people such as Jeffrey Sachs, the economist who serves as a special advisor to the UN Secretary General. His position (now the plug) has been documented several times in the Social Marketing In the News section of my blog: He would prefer to see it banned when it comes to asking people to pay for mosquito nets – regardless of the price.

Bottom line: Your theoretical or philosophical model for how behavior comes to be, is maintained and can be most effectively modified or changed determines how you use the principles and tools that social marketing provides. This was always the central point of people like Larry Wallack and other proponents of a social determinant point-of-view who criticized social marketing for 'blaming the victim.' Individual theories of behavior change will lead you down that path, whether you utilize a social marketing approach or some other model. The rise of social ecological models, policy interventions and environmental change approaches to public health are all attempts to reorient how 'we' view the world and interact with it in our professional capacities. In the way I think about social marketing, it provides a systematic and strategic way to think about issues of being audience-centric, aware of and responsive to larger trends and competition in the environment, using research to guide and inform program development, and applying the 4Ps. The more theoretical models we have in our toolboxes to bring to the task, the more successful, I believe, we will be.

Notes
1. http://www.economist.com/research/Economics/alphabetic.
    cfm?term=economics
2. http://www.russellsage.org/programs/other/behavioral/
3. Bloom, PN and Novelli, WD. (1981). Problems and challenges in social
    marketing. *Journal of Marketing*;**45**:79-88.

10 Ways to Be the Smartest Social Marketer in the Room

Social marketing continues to inspire me when I witness how a few simple questions and acts can help people focus on important strategic issues and work together to improve people's lives. When we first published *Strategic Questions for Consumer-Based Health Communications*[1] (don't let the title fool you, all three authors are bona fide social marketers), I would tell my staff that it contained 7 questions they should use in every program planning meeting. Those questions and a few simple acts prove, time and again, to be world-changing for participants in these meetings. Here they are:

1. **Who will be the target consumers and what are they like?** To answer this question one must do empirical research on consumers to describe those who are possible targets and then select the consumer segment likely to achieve the greatest gains toward the public health objective. Target selection is based on several factors: the size of the consumer segment (the number of people the program is trying to reach); the extent to which the consumer segment needs or would benefit from the behavior change (for example, incidence of morbidity and mortality); how reachable they are with available resources (accessibility); and the extent to which they are likely to respond to communications (responsiveness).

2. I also encourage you to think more broadly and more deeply about audience segmentation and priority-setting by asking the question: **Who is critical to the success of the program?** Social marketers usually rely on other people or groups to implement various parts of the program (peer influentials, intermediary organizations, media representatives). At other times, policy makers or senior managers may be key determinants for the long term sustainability of a social marketing effort. Yet, rarely do I see program designers explicitly focus a marketing strategy on these types of audiences despite their often critical role in accomplishing the goals of the program.

3. **What action should the target person take as a direct result of the communication?** This question aims at choosing the consumer's action after the communication. This action may differ from the public health objective, the recommended behavior that is based on clinical and epidemiologic research. The "science" may say people should stop smoking or get a mammogram or

eat five or more daily servings of fruits and vegetables. But just telling people to do something ignores where they are coming from or how they can get to the recommended behavior. Effective communication requires an understanding of the target's behavior process, a "map" of the steps along the way to or from the healthy behavior.

4. **What reward should the message promise the consumer?** This question focuses the team on which rewards the target consumer might find most appealing and motivating. A consumer reward is a future gain resulting from the action. It is not limited to scientific facts or other objective realities, but it exists in the mind of the consumer, and often, the consumer dispenses the reward to himself or herself.

5. **How can the promise be made credible?** It is one task to promise the consumer a competitive reward; it is another to make the promise credible. Support can come from relevant information about the behavior and from how the message is presented - its execution. Scientific facts about the recommended behavior change can supply the informational support if the facts are important, understandable, and believable to the consumer, as well as unique to the behavior compared with its competitors. A thoroughly research-based description of the consumer will prove its value again by providing information on the relevance and believability of such facts.

6. **What communication openings and vehicles should be used?** Consumers' minds are closed to the message by selective inattention and selective perception. Yet in the right frame of mind, they are more apt to notice, attend to, and act favorably on messages that meet their needs. So, consumer-based health communication seeks the openings in the person's life and the vehicles that best fit through those openings. The openings are the times, places, and circumstances in which the consumer is most receptive to the message.

7. **What image should distinguish the action?** All but the newest behaviors already have an image - a set of expectations and associated feelings among consumers. The image of the action may be positive, neutral, or negative, it may be more or less crystallized, and it may be simple or complicated. The action's image is like a personality: its elements or traits are mutually consistent,

it endures over time, it is unique, it heightens perceptions that are consistent with it, and it encourages people to ignore or discount perceptions that are inconsistent with it. Today I usually talk about this in terms of a brand for the behavior – but if people are more comfortable with image, go with it! The issues and outcomes are the same.

8. **Always be the <u>audience advocate</u> in the room.** Don't let the professionals or do-gooders get away with ideology, scientific facts, 'gut feelings' and past practices as the reason for program strategy and tactics. What makes behavior change work or not is how well the proposed behaviors (adopting new ones, not adopting or quitting others) fit the reality of the audience. If the people formerly known as the audience are not in the room representing themselves and co-creating the program (a practice I strongly endorse), then the social marketer needs to represent their point-of-view as best they can (and if you can't, do your research!).

9. **Assume a role in the group that confronts the devil's advocate(s) in the group at every turn.** I particularly like The Anthropologist and The Experimenter from Tom Kelley's *The Ten Faces of Innovation*[3]. Tom calls the Anthropologist role 'the single biggest source of innovation at IDEO.' The Experimenter focuses on the prototype building – or the 'test it and see' approach rather than giving into ideological and intellectual bull shitake. The Anthropologist goes into the field for answers and to experience what is really happening (rather than visiting the zoo or relying on the filtered views of others).

10. **Focus on "Getting Together"[2] rather than "Getting to Yes."** <u>Behavior change starts with the planning group – the first priority audience that is key to success</u>. What you believe are the important steps and processes to get to an effective program are not going to be shared with many others – at least at the beginning. You can try to be the persuasive, dictatorial, dominating, highhanded or authoritative manager of the group. However, you will find more long-term success by being the negotiator between factions (though the short-term consequences may have you thinking twice). Another book that should be on every social marketer's reading table and a set of tools for every social marketer's toolbox.

Notes
1. Sutton, S.M., Balch, G.I., Lefebvre R.C. Strategic questions for consumer-based health communications. *Public Health Reports*, 1995;**110**:725–33.
2. Fisher, R., Brown, S. *Getting Together: Building Relationships as We Negotiate*. New York: Penguin Books, 1989.
3. Kelley, T., Littman, J. *The Ten Faces of Innovation: IDEO's Strategies for Defeating the Devil's Advocate and Driving Creativity Throughout Your Organization*. New York: Random House, 2005.

Conversation with Richard Pollard

I was delighted to have Richard Pollard accept an invitation to join our *Conversations on Social Marketing* this past week [George Washington University School of Public Health, 6 November 2007]. I had met him in the past few months and quickly found not only a fount of colorful stories from the earliest days of social marketing, but one of the most innovative thinkers in focusing on the role of social marketing in the health marketplace.

Today, Richard may be best known for his contributions to the development of the Total Market Approach (TMA) which has spawned some corollary movements including Making Markets Work for the Poor.[1] TMA isn't something you'll find in any of the social marketing texts, and indeed, it seems to be known and discussed by only a few in the international development field, including at the Center for Global Development and private sector development staff at The World Bank. However, he clearly showed its evolutionary arc from the first social marketing projects of the 1970s, and their even earlier progenitors - social responsibility campaigns in India in the 1960s. Part history lesson, and part glimpse into the future, Richard provided an impressive and thorough introduction to some ideas you will be hearing more about in the years to come.

The presentation began with the recognition that *behavior change programs that require a product or service to ensure compliance must ensure these services are available, accessible and affordable.* BUT… there are often inadequate public sector resources to achieve equitable coverage and sustain it; donor fatigue at continuing to put funds into the same programs for years if not decades; and the unmet needs of substantial segments of the population even after implementation occurs that are often related to access issues and existing realities.

One of the more important slides Richard showed was a chart depicting the relative *share of pocketbook* that people spend in countries such as Kenya, Cambodia, Egypt, India and China. In all instances, *more than 50% of people's health expenditures are in the private sector and in no case did health expenditures in the public sector reach 40%.* His point is that there is already a fragmented marketplace for health products and services that is by its very nature inequitable (it favors people who can afford to pay for products and services even in societies that are, in theory and by design, suppose to provide public services to everyone). The development of the TMA approach is, in part, an attempt to correct some of these marketplace inequities and develop more sustainable long-term solutions to health problems.

Richard defined TMA as one in which all sectors (public, private and NGO or donor-financed social marketing) are integrated within one "market" that is segmented by willingness to pay. The objective is to open up the market to the commercial sector through better targeting of public and NGO/social marketing subsidies to the poorest of the poor and allowing the commercial sector to develop products and services to other groups more able and willing to pay [Ed Note: see for example *The Next 4 Billion*[2]]. The overriding issue confronting TMA approaches is to ensure total market growth and rural/low-income access that gains more users and, therefore, increased volume through rural wholesalers and community-based distribution. A TMA approach must also insure that commercial interests are not squeezed out of the market (whether it be for condoms, oral contraceptives or LLINs) by free or very low cost public or subsidized social marketing supply to those who can afford mass market prices and are willing to pay. Finally, there must be in place a fair regulatory and policy playing field.

He identified the roles of social marketing organizations (SMOs) in TMA as:

- Assisting all sectors to move to a TMA over time.
- Selling commodities to achieve a behavioral result.
- Helping the public sector achieve better targeting of subsidies, and implementing cost recovery as appropriate.
- Regarding their own brands as a strategy to open up markets for future commercial sector.
- Supporting national, integrated demand generation activities across all sectors.
- Motivating the commercial sector to re-price brands and modulating product price subsidies where required (LLINs or ACT).
- Developing community-based initiatives linking communications with the provision of commodities.
- Pursuing public-sector and NGO-sector outreach.
- Exploring and implementing micro-credit and other BOTP approaches[3].
- Creating adequate demand on rural kiosks/shops.

TMA will only work well when driven by consumer demand and choice. He pointed out that consumers are more than willing to pay whatever they can afford. A payment adds value! There are also no quick fixes for a market. One low cost brand cannot make a market; it requires multiple brands and pricing coupled with strong demand. Finally, an equitable market is one where all sectors of society have access to a range of brands they can afford and market subsidies/distortions are carefully targeted. To my way of thinking, all the types of activities social marketers who understand the role of markets in health behavior change may be among the best to plan and undertake.

With his closing slide, Richard made the following points:

- Most markets are unique and are at different levels of maturity.
- Notably, public sector policies/capacities are different; existing demand levels are different.
- The role of an SMO is to (1) identify strategies to move towards a TMA over a realistic time-frame and establish its own strategies and (2) establish market positioning of their own brands and policies within that framework for each country.
- The role of donors is to work within long-term market development scenarios.

The next time you hear someone talk about upstream approaches to public health, ask yourself if they have reached the core and identified the strength of the social marketing approach: competing in and harmonizing the marketplace of behaviors, ideas, products and services.

Notes
1. http://www.dfidhealthrc.org/publications/srh/SM_review_Sept03.pdf
2. *The Next 4 Billion: Market Size and Business Strategy at the Base of the Pyramid.* http://www.wri.org/publication/the-next-4-billion
3. http://en.wikipedia.org/wiki/Bottom_of_the_Pyramid

Social Marketing, Total Market
Approach and the Base of the Pyramid

I was asked to contribute an article to a special issue of *Effective Executive* on BOP Markets and Strategies. The issue explores different perspectives on the ideas popularized by CK Prahalad in *The Fortune at the Bottom of the Pyramid*. He argues that there is much untapped purchasing power among the world's poor, and that companies can make significant profits by selling to the poor with business models adapted to this unique market. Through selling to the poor, private companies can also bring prosperity to them and thus act as a positive force in alleviating poverty.

His challenge to focus on the BOP market has been taken up by many multinational companies and social entrepreneurs with numerous books and articles appearing in the business and popular press documenting the interest (see for example Kash Rangan et al *Business Solutions for the Global Poor*, Stuart Hart's *Capitalism at the Crossroads*, and Ted London's *BOP Perspective on Poverty Alleviation*.)

My contribution, *Strategies for the Base of the Pyramid: Lessons from Social Marketing*, introduces social marketing and the work that has been done in this marketplace for over 3 decades. My point is that there is a great degree of overlap in purpose and approach of social marketing and BOP efforts, and much that can be learned and shared between us. I believe that the BOP movement can be an impetus to even better social marketing and that social marketing can give creative capitalists [See *Creative Capitalism and Social Marketing*] a jump-start in understanding and working in the BOP marketplace. We should be working to bring these worlds together with a Total Market Approach [See *Conversation with Richard Pollard*]. Two excerpts from the article:

"The four billion people at the base of the economic pyramid (BOP) - all those with incomes below $3,000 in local purchasing power - live in relative poverty. Yet, together they have substantial purchasing power: the BOP constitutes a $5 trillion global consumer market. It tends to be concentrated in rural areas, especially in Asia. As a consequence, these markets are usually very poorly served, dominated by an informal economy, and, as a result, relatively inefficient and uncompetitive."

Hammond et al make the argument that the BOP should be the focus of businesses seeking to expand into new markets. As opposed to more traditional aid programs in developing countries that are mediated or directed by governments and non-governmental organizations (NGOs), a private sector-driven, market-based approach needs to focus as much on people as producers as well as consumers, and on solutions that can make markets more efficient, competitive, and inclusive...

The TMA approach has evolved out of more than 30 years of experience conducting social marketing programs in developing countries among people now described as the BOP market. The approach has much in common with the current BOP market analysis activities, and the market-based approach to poverty reduction. Both the TMA and BOP approaches reinforce an approach to poverty reduction that is framed in terms of enabling opportunity and less in terms of aid. A successful market-based approach would bring significant new private sector resources into play, allowing development assistance to be more targeted to the segments and sectors for which no viable market solutions can presently be found. As the TMA approach says, the active entry of the private sector into providing goods and services to the poor needs to be supported, but their work needs to be assessed and evaluated in the larger context of the marketplace. This assessment needs to be focused on how the public, NGO and private sectors contribute by their unique and complimentary strengths to attain equitable, efficient, sustainable and affordable health and health care across the population."

Creative Capitalism and Social Marketing

Bill Gates recently called for a revision of capitalism *to make the aspects of capitalism that serve wealthier people serve poorer people as well.*[1] In his speech at The 2008 World Economic Forum in Davos, he outlined **creative capitalism** this way:

Such a system would have a twin mission: making profits and also improving lives for those who don't fully benefit from market forces. To make the system sustainable, we need to use profit incentives whenever we can.

At the same time, profits are not always possible when business tries to serve the very poor. In such cases, there needs to be another market-based incentive - and that incentive is recognition. Recognition enhances a company's reputation and appeals to customers; above all, it attracts good people to the organization. As such, recognition triggers a market-based reward for good behavior. In markets where profits are not possible, recognition is a proxy; where profits are possible, recognition is an added incentive.

The challenge is to design a system where market incentives, including profits and recognition, drive the change...

This kind of creative capitalism matches business expertise with needs in the developing world to find markets that are already there, but are untapped. Sometimes market forces fail to make an impact in developing countries not because there's no demand, or because money is lacking, but because we don't spend enough time studying the needs and limits of that market.

The speech has touched off a number of conversations, including one convened last week at the Hudson Institute - *Creative capitalism: Can it meet the needs of the world's poor*. Ryan Baebler at NextBillion.net provides a summary of the discussion.[2]

I was also at the meeting and here are some of my notes.

This isn't the first time self-interest and social interest have been combined in a new form of capitalism - Bill Schambra.

Bill Easterly identified two problems with this formulation of creative capitalism: (1) it provides weak incentives for the private sector to do things differently (i.e., if recognition is the goal, might corporations decide to provide goods and services that get the broadest media coverage rather than what does the most good and is responsive to the needs of the poor?), and (2) it doesn't address the question of choosing which goods to give to the poor (for example, with limited resources do you expend them on antiretrovirals for people with AIDS or a basic health package of oral rehydration therapy, antibiotics, nutrition supplements and vaccines that would save 10 million lives a year).

His position is *capitalism may be one of the worst ways to reduce poverty, except for everything else that has been tried.* The right answer, he states, is to <u>enable the poor to pay for whatever goods they decide they need most and not have them continue to depend on someone to give it to them for free.</u>

Al Hammond directed attention to the divisions at Microsoft, Intel and other companies that are devoted to identifying needs of the poorest and innovating products and services that meet those needs as examples of what Gates calls for in his speech.

He talked of the need to understand base of the pyramid (BOP) markets and referred to the recent report on The Next 4 Billion marketplace[3] that, I believe, should be required reading for anyone working in this area. He focused on the implications of the report for health and access to essential products and services and how the proliferation of mobile phones at the BOP (something I have been talking about here as well) offers new ways to think about programs and interventions. His take on paying for products and services is that *the evidence is people are willing to pay if it enhances their productivity and economic well-being.*

Some of his other research suggests that access is the most important issue for people at the BOP; they spend more on getting to health services and products than the actual goods themselves.

Later, in response to a question about strengthening public-private partnerships, Al made the point that the public sector often doesn't know how to harness the profit motive to achieve its goals. Indeed, the mistrust with which both the public and NGO sectors view the private sector is one of the greatest impediments to moving to action. Bill Easterly called these partnerships *the latest fad in development* and wondered whether the public and private sector really have the same objectives in these partnerships.

During the past week, I also had a reporter contact me asking about *the implications of creative capitalism for social marketing.* He sent me four questions that I have paraphrased below and include for your inspection the answers I sent back to him [note: this was prior to the Hudson meeting].

1. What does this mean for Africa?

It helps set an agenda for people to think and talk about development issues in Africa - and indeed around the world - in an innovative way. Let's move beyond partnerships to ask how the role of governments, civil society and corporations can change to expand the reach of market forces to serve all people in need. I hope it flips the conversation from asking whether the private sector should be more effectively engaged in development issues to how? How do we innovate and adapt those aspects of markets that work so well for so many of us to work as well for the next billion people on earth who live on less than a dollar a day?

2. Is it a new idea or a retread?

I believe it reinforces, among other things, the need to focus on private sector values such as speed and efficiency in more of our work. I see it as an approach that can embrace the ideas of Bill Easterly in supporting the urgency to search for new approaches to aid, and to do that *we need to understand markets and the people they serve in a truly market-driven sense where the people participate in shaping their own destiny*. George Ayittey talks about the 'cheetahs' - the new breed of African he describes as not wanting to wait for governments to decide on how to solve problems.[4] These social entrepreneurs can be inspired to make change by new ways of thinking about capitalism. After all, he points out, markets existed in Africa long before the colonialists arrived.

The other trends I see this tying into are recent work on 'the next 4 billion market' and efforts to measure the business opportunities at the base of the pyramid (BOP) and the Total Market Approach that is evolving out of social marketing [See *Social Marketing Approach, Total Market Approach and Social Marketing*].

3. Will corporations listen?

I expect that when Bill Gates talks in Davos they listen. The question is whether they will act. And as Bill points out in his speech, whether they do so or not is contingent in some respects on how governments (and large donors) set policy and disburse funds to create market incentives for companies to improve the lives of the poor.

4. Does it (implicitly) endorse a social marketing approach?

The idea of creative capitalism moves in a similar direction to where some of us in social marketing are going; a total market approach where the public, NGO and private sectors work together to expand the reach of market forces to serve all people in need. <u>TMA recognizes the power of markets to bring dignity and choice to the everyday lives of all people, regardless of their current ability to access or pay for essential health information, products and services. It is when barriers are lowered, and opportunities increased, that choosing to act in ways that lead to meaningful changes in one's own life are possible. Markets have a major role to play in making that happen.</u>

Notes

1. http://online.wsj.com/public/article_print/SBI20II3473219511791.
   html
2. http://www.nextbillion.net/blog/2008/02/02/the-week-went-well
3. http://www.wri.org/publication/the-next-4-billion
4. http://www.ted.com/talks/george_ayittey_on_cheetahs_vs_hippos.html

Comparative Effectiveness Research and Social Marketing

Comparative Effectiveness Research (CER) is one of the buzzwords in the health care reform and economic stimulus package conversations in which $1.1 billion is allocated for CER.

CER studies offer the opportunity to evaluate social marketing under more rigorous conditions than are typically present in our applied work. Yet, one danger is that many policy staff, grant makers and investigators will mistakenly operationalize the term 'social marketing' to include interventions that only use communication strategies or only sell products to consumers. I hope funders of CER research, and the policy makers, will educate themselves that social marketing is more than either of those extremes, and that incentive systems coupled with better access and improved opportunities for more people to lead healthier lives are part of the social marketing mix and the CER that is eventually funded.

The Institute of Medicine (IOM) just released their list of the 100 national priority areas for CER.[1] I have pulled from their list some examples where social marketing should be at the table.

1. Compare the effectiveness of primary prevention methods, such as exercise and balance training, versus clinical treatments in preventing falls in older adults at varying degrees of risk.
2. Compare the effectiveness of dissemination and translation techniques to facilitate the use of CER by patients, clinicians, payers, and others.
3. Compare the effectiveness and costs of alternative detection and management strategies (e.g., pharmacologic treatment, social/family support, combined pharmacologic and social/family support) for dementia in community-dwelling individuals and their caregivers.
4. Compare the effectiveness of school-based interventions involving meal programs, vending machines, and physical education, at different levels of intensity, in preventing and treating overweight and obesity in children and adolescents.
5. Compare the effectiveness of various strategies (e.g., clinical interventions, selected social interventions [such as improving the built environment in communities and making healthy foods more available], combined clinical and social interventions) to prevent obesity, hypertension, diabetes, and

heart disease in at-risk populations such as the urban poor and American Indians.

6. Compare the effectiveness of the various delivery models (e.g., primary care, dental offices, schools, mobile vans) in preventing dental caries in children.

7. Compare the effectiveness of wraparound home and community-based services and residential treatment in managing serious emotional disorders in children and adults.

8. Compare the effectiveness of interventions (e.g., community-based multi-level interventions, simple health education, usual care) to reduce health disparities in cardiovascular disease, diabetes, cancer, musculoskeletal diseases, and birth outcomes.

9. Compare the effectiveness of literacy-sensitive disease management programs and usual care in reducing disparities in children and adults with low literacy and chronic disease (e.g., heart disease).

10. Compare the effectiveness of clinical interventions (e.g., prenatal care, nutritional counseling, smoking cessation, substance abuse treatment, and combinations of these interventions) to reduce incidences of infant mortality, pre-term births, and low birth rates, especially among African American women.

11. Compare the effectiveness of innovative strategies for preventing unintended pregnancies (e.g., over-the-counter access to oral contraceptives or other hormonal methods, expanding access to long-acting methods for young women, providing free contraceptive methods at public clinics, pharmacies, or other locations).

12. Compare the effectiveness of strategies for enhancing patients' adherence to medication regimens.

13. Compare the effectiveness of patient decision support tools on informing diagnostic and treatment decisions (e.g., treatment choice, knowledge acquisition, treatment-preference concordance, decisional conflict) for elective surgical and nonsurgical procedures—especially in patients with limited English-language proficiency, limited education, hearing or visual impairments, or mental health problems.

And those are from just the first 30 or so top priorities - you get the idea.

I know that some social marketers will shudder at the idea of pigeon-holing social marketing programs into randomized clinical trials. For them, and other readers, I suggest you take a look at an article in the Annals of Internal Medicine by Luce et al (2009) *Rethinking randomized clinical trials for comparative effectiveness research: The need for transformational change.*[2] Their thesis is:

…many RCTs as currently designed and conducted are ill suited to meet the evidentiary needs implicit in the IOM definition of CER: comparison of effective interventions among patients in typical patient care settings, with decisions tailored to individual patient needs. Without major changes in how we conceive, design, conduct, and analyze RCTs, the nation risks spending large sums of money inefficiently to answer the wrong questions—or the right questions too late.

My point is that there are many ways in which social marketing can be the subject of pragmatic research studies and applied to the solution of many challenges facing the health of Americans and the people who care about them. What are you doing to insure that society benefits from all that we have been learning in social marketing over the past 25 years?

Notes
1. http://www.iom.edu/Reports/2009/ComparativeEffectivenessResearch-Priorities.aspx
2. http://www.annals.org/content/151/3/206.full

The People Formerly Known as the Audience

I'm in an Audience State-of-Mind

When I look at how many of us use the term 'audience,' I conjure an image of a passive, shiftless, group who are waiting to be persuaded (about something), entertained (by something), engaged (with something) or encouraged (to do something). This image has a direct effect on how I think about my social marketing and health communication efforts: do I inform? Amuse? Create interesting products and services? Get emotional? Or some combination of them?

When I think about people, I construct a sense of groups that are striving to accomplish things (if just to survive the day), aspiring to better lives, seeking solutions to their problems and constructively interacting with others. My social marketing program might then revolve around: How can I be relevant in their lives? Help them reach their goals? Solve their problems (not mine, the organization's or society's)? Interact more effectively with others? [Some might refer to these as 'adding value;' - I agree. I just like to move beyond the vague.]

The details of the answers to these questions lie in our ability to communicate and empathize (NOT sympathize) with people formerly known as the audience. But those are the wrong questions for today.

Rather, seeing people as active and creative actors in their own lives, and not passive recipients of their fate - or what **we** do, sets the tone for how we each respectively approach our social role. When I am an **audience** I DO want to be entertained, satisfied immediately and left alone in my experience of the moment (try interrupting THAT!). When I am **the change agent** I want to disrupt this perceived passivity, challenge the 'satisfied now' and stimulate experiences of social solidarity and action.

I choose to create relevance and immediacy in their lives with meaningful ideas and experiences.

I desire to create thoughtfulness and passion to bring people fully in touch with their beliefs and motives and act on them responsibly (yes, that's opening a debate).

I aspire to create hope that their lives can be better (however each of us defines it), our institutions can improve and the world can be a better place too - and that we can find ways to do just that.

I want to shift the dominant social forces that preach ideas and behaviors such as 'consume and die;' 'be still, be quiet, be docile;' and 'be easy, fun and popular.'

Most of all, I want to do it as **us** - not **to** them, **at** them or **for** them.

We talk about the changing role of the audience and the emerging role of the change agent; should we talk more about **the us of change**?

Segmentation: The First Critical Decision

I suspect that more time is given to debates over whether and how to segment an audience than to any other decision made in a social marketing program. And for good reason. The process of segmentation distills the aspirations and predilections of stakeholders and designers into an essence that will (or a least should) permeate every aspect of the program.

Audience segmentation operates from the principle that "birds of a feather flock together." Each of these flocks share certain characteristics whether they be sociodemographic or psychographic (or choose your own). However, each flock is distinct from the others based on other variables. What we are doing in social marketing is trying to figure which flocks are most important to target to improve public health and social welfare, usually around a specific topic (breast cancer prevention, recycling, participating in mentoring programs). In the marketing business, these flocks often go by the name of "target audiences." While the notion of a "target" makes sense in the militaristic jargon that permeates marketing, I often find that the term "priority audience" gives a sense of reassurance to practitioners and stakeholders that we are not somehow dehumanizing the people we serve and, on the other hand, recognizes that - as in all things - priorities (including audiences) can shift over time.

Many writers in the social marketing world (including myself) have advocated for the creative use of many different types of segmentation strategies to design programs with more relevance, greater reach and increased effectiveness. Indeed, the mainstream thinking among commercial marketers today is to aim for the "audience of one" through what is known as mass customization. Whether or not this segmentation strategy will prove practical and effective for social marketers remains to be seen. However, what is often a reality for most social marketing programs is that limited data about priority audiences, the lack of expertise in using multivariate statistical analyses to develop segmentation categories, resource restrictions that hamper the tailoring of the marketing mix to multiple audiences, and mandates to achieve impact across a broad swath of the population make the use of sophisticated and fine-tuned segmentation strategies difficult to implement.

In some of the recent work I have been doing, we have been looking at the question of audience segmentation from the perspective of addressing three basic questions:

Who are the people at highest risk? This question is designed to mine the demographic and epidemiological data that are often the only ones available to program designers. The answers to this question can then be combined with other data collected during the formative research process to identify one or more groups of possible priority audiences.

Who are the people most open to change? From among the groups identified in response to the first question it makes sense from both a theoretical perspective (e.g., diffusion of innovations, stages of change) and a practical one to focus our initial efforts on those subgroups that are more predisposed or motivated to engage in new behaviors.

Who are the people/groups critical to the success of the program? Social marketers usually rely on other people or groups to implement various parts of the program (peer influentials, intermediary organizations, media representatives). At other times, policy makers or senior managers may be key determinants for the long term sustainability of a social marketing effort. Yet, rarely do I see program designers explicitly focus a marketing strategy on these types of audiences despite their often critical role in accomplishing the goals of the program.

Depending on the marketing (behavioral or social change) objectives of the program, there may be more than one answer to each of these three questions. What we often find in going through this exercise is that question #2 (who is most open to change) usually fine tunes the choices made to question #1. While this 2-step process is the more obvious part of segmentation, I will submit that it is in the ignoring of the last question where most programs discover (too late) their plan's Achilles' heel.

Rediscovering Market Segmentation – Part I

The February 2006 issue of *Harvard Business Review* includes an article[1] that I highly recommend to all social marketers and health communicators. After calling upon companies for market segmentation strategies that went beyond simple demographics over 40 years ago (a call that many of us in social marketing have also made over the years as well), the authors note:

Market segmentation has become narrowly focused on the needs of advertising, which it serves mainly by populating commercials with characters that viewers can identify with – the marketing equivalent of central casting…The idea was to broaden the use of segmentation so that it could inform not just advertising but also product innovation, pricing, choice of distribution channels, and the like.

Their central point is that market segmentation should be helping marketers figure out and decide what types of products and services they should be offering to various consumer groups or audience segments. In the social marketing vernacular, we would be talking about what types of behaviors (and products and services perhaps) we should be offering to various <u>priority audiences</u> (See *Segmentation: The First Critical Decision*) and not who or what should be featured on our posters or PSAs (and those 'rainbow' characters are always a giveaway that that was EXACTLY what the segmentation discussion was about – central casting). The problem is that most segmentation work isn't done with behavioral features in mind - the actual characteristics of what we are asking people to do. At best, much of this research simply focuses on explanatory variables (knowledge, attitudes and beliefs being primary ones of interest) that satisfy curiosity, but leave behavioral objectives fairly murky.

The authors add that *Good segmentations identify the groups most worth pursuing – the underserved, the dissatisfied, and those likely to make a first-time purchase.* Add words like high risk, disenfranchised and contemplators and they might as well be speaking to social marketers. As I read that last quote, I was reminded of an article Bill Novelli wrote several years ago in which he pointed out that many of the so-called 'guerilla marketing'[2] techniques that were coming into vogue among the commercial marketers were strategies and tactics many of us in the social marketing world had been using for years. While there is a consistent call for social marketing's need to adopt from the commercial sector, it is always interesting to stop and note that cross-fertilization is possible - whether consciously or not.

[N.B.: What would happen if more commercial marketers were aware of social marketing theories and practices? Hint: The answer is not better corporate social responsibility programs.]

This is also a good place to stop and address the question that regular readers of this blog might have: what about <u>audience insights</u>? (See: *Aspiring to Audience Insights — Part A*) A good question that reflects a tendency of program designers to combine segmentation and audience research into the same step — what is often called 'exploratory research.' For example, a program planning group might choose to conduct focus groups with 12-16 year-old girls about physical activity knowledge, attitudes and behaviors, and then afterwards divide them into two segments of 12-14 year-olds and 15-16 year-olds based on some insight from the groups (e.g., girls in high school think about this issue a lot differently than girls in elementary school grades). What is left undone in this example is to understand what may appeal to and motivate each group of girls to be more physically active. A better approach might be to make segmentation decisions before sponsoring primary research activities by reviewing other research on the subject, or if they had the time and resources, a more thorough research effort first focused on key segmentation issues (see the next installment for six questions Y&M suggest we consider when planning segmentation studies). Then they could explore the subject with homogeneous groups and focus on insight as the objective of the focus group studies, not segmentation criteria.

Notes
1. Yankelovich, D., Meer, D. Rediscovering market segmentation. *Harvard Business Review*, 2006 (February). Available at: http://www.viewpointlearning. org/publications/articles/segmentation_0206.pdf
2. http://en.wikipedia.org/wiki/Guerilla_marketing

Rediscovering Market Segmentation – Part 2

Picking up from the preceding section, Part 1, the second part of the Yankelovich & Meer article in the *Harvard Business Review* ['Rediscovering Market Segmentation'] includes their recommendations for six questions to ask yourself when you are developing your segmentation scheme.

What are we trying to do? Audience research is not about exploring the personalities of priority audiences (or any of a host of variables that hold more theoretical than practical value), but identifying groups of people open to trying the behaviors we are suggesting to them. If, say, we want to increase physical activity among 12-16 year-old girls, then segmentation strategies might focus on which subgroups of these girls are more open to being active alone or with others, want structured activities or convenience, or were more active when they were younger.

Which customers drive profits? That is, which priority audiences matter to and impact on an organization's ability to meet its mission and objectives. For example, while many programs focus on 'new' adopters for target behaviors, it may actually be more profitable (achieve better reach and higher levels of efficiency and efficacy) in some circumstances to focus on "current" adopters who are asked to serve as the models and promoters for the behavior (the community health worker movement has certainly been successful with this approach for over 20 years).

Which attitudes matter to the buying decision? Focusing on what Yankelovich & Meer term "immutable personality traits" does not mean that lifestyles, attitudes, self-image and aspirations cannot be explored with potential audiences, just that these explorations be related to the behaviors (products or services) we are interested in offering, increasing or decreasing. Thus, for our 12-16 year-old girls, understanding that the change from elementary or middle school to high school has a number of impacts on self-esteem and social status; that striving for autonomy and independence from family influences increases over this age range; and that these girls lead overscheduled, hectic lives in which they believe they 'need more energy' to get through the day are important as long as they relate to understanding the context for increasing physical activity and suggesting elements of the marketing mix on which to base our intervention strategies.

What are my customers actually doing? Yankelovich & Meer point to the enduring psychological principle that the best predictor of future behavior is one's past behavior as a reminder that formative research should strive to create conditions or simulations for the audience to respond to as often as is feasible. For physical activity we might ask these girls to keep a daily log for a week prior to the focus group session to record times and places where they thought they might have been able to be more active "if only... [fill in the blank]." Or we could ask them to take photos with disposable cameras or their cell phones of areas around their home or school neighborhoods that are 'great,' 'bad,' and 'could be made better' places to be physically active and then discuss these photos and 'reasons why' in any of a variety of formats (individual interviews, dyads or triads).

Will this segmentation make sense to senior management? A point I don't often see made about segmentation schemes but, as Yankelovich & Meer illustrate, can be a real stumbling block for marketing managers in proposing new programs. I can imagine what some public health officials have thought (if not said out loud) when presented with segmentations that went beyond the 'known and safe' demographic world. And I have been asked on occasion by leery senior managers to provide a reality check on their staff's proposed segmentation strategy. Finally, imagine the resistance of managers who don't trust the research designs, methods or data analytic techniques because they are unfamiliar with them?

Can our segmentation register change? Their point here is that segmentations should not be viewed as one-time, go-for-broke activities but as part of on-going research efforts to address important organizational questions and public health/social change issues. Not only can an 'all-or-nothing' approach be a barrier to reaching consensus on priority audiences, (*see: "Segmentation: The First Critical Decision"*) but it also undermines the important role and contribution this research makes to the overall program.

The takeaway from this article for social marketers and health communicators:
How to Tell That Your Segmentation Scheme Needs Work

- It reads like a page from a census document.
- It is overly concerned with the consumers' identities to the neglect of which behavioral features matter to current and potential audiences (for physical activity - what types of activities, under what circumstances, for how long, when and with whom are some of the features that can be considered).

- There is too little emphasis on the actual behaviors of the audience (these are the audience profiles where you feel all 'warm and fuzzy' about the audience but don't have a clue about what they do when it comes to engaging in the target behaviors or any of the possible competitive ones).
- There is too much attention given to the technical details of creating the segmentation scheme that raise significant questions from the decision makers who have the ultimate sign off authority.
- There are no obvious implications for how to position the desired behavior versus competing ones, what incentives to offer, what barriers to address, where and when to provide opportunities to try and/or engage in the behavior, and what promotional strategies and messages may be most relevant for the audience.
- Remember that insight *(see: "Aspiring to Audience Insights Part A and B")* is the **next** step.

Aspiring to Audience Insights – Part A

Two of the books that appear among my "Recommended Reads" are there because they discuss a subject and process that is rarely reflected in the work of social marketers and health communicators. While we all profess to the canon of identifying and understanding our target audiences, the audience research that is conducted to build a foundation for the program often misses the mark. The reason why is described from the perspective of the Account Planner in _Truth, Lies and Advertising_ and the Creative Director in _Then We Set His Hair on Fire_. BTW – two positions you rarely see on social marketing and health communication "teams" unless advertising agencies are involved in the project.

Jon Steele sets out to demonstrate that _The best and most effective advertising [read 'social marketing/health communications'] is that which sets out to involve consumers, both in its communication and in the process of developing its message._ He views the account planner's role as not just the person responsible for "embracing" consumers in the process (rather than shepherding them into focus group rooms), but using their input to inform and inspire the entire creative process and then guide and validate the resulting campaign. You might think of the planner as the formative and process research guru who knows how to think and talk in creativese. Jon's key point, and one that we practiced at Prospect Associates religiously (as many of our clients can attest to), was the use of research to reach a creative brief. And that research had to be focused on one objective: uncovering a consumer insight that informs all aspects of the communications and marketing program. For example, in the truth®campaign[1], the essential audience insight is described in their identity brochure as:

truth® taps into the natural rebel in most teens and alerts them to the misleading marketing tactics of the tobacco industry, encouraging teens to be wary consumers that resist this deadly product.

Note that the insight does not explicitly describe marketing strategies or communication tactics. What it does provide is a transformative platform for creative people to tackle preventing tobacco use among youth. It immediately shifted not just this campaign, but many similar efforts, once and for all from preaching the dangers of tobacco smoking to pointing out the evils of the tobacco companies in a way that enhanced personal relevance and inclinations and behaviors to not smoke among the priority audience.

What sets this approach to audience insight apart from more traditional approaches to audience 'understanding' is (a) the "rules" for conducting audience research aren't followed [and you know what they are!], (b) the questions are posed to get audience input and not confirmation of planners' opinions, and (c) the results are analyzed by people looking for insights - not means, modes and medians [and you know who they are too!].

However, striving for insight that informs creative program development and actually achieving it are two different things. Compare this statement with the one from truth® and then think about which creative director you'd rather be.

Messages for tweens should focus on helping tweens discover their passion. Tweens are engaged by messages of self-discovery and seeking out their identity. Both involved and uninvolved youth are attracted to self-discovery messages and, more importantly, want to feel good about themselves. Involvement in activities must be positioned as a vehicle for self-discovery and self-esteem enhancement. Additionally, the idea that everyone is good at something will be an important motivational message for uninvolved youth with lower self-esteem.

Next: a view from the director's chair.

Note
1. http://www.legacyforhealth.org

Aspiring to Audience Insights – Part B

Despite its title, <u>Then We Set His Hair on Fire</u> [a reference to an accident that occurred on the set while shooting a Pepsi ad featuring Michael Jackson], this book is not advertising industry war stories but a paean to insight as the driving force behind all great advertising – and I would add, all great social marketing. The author, Phil Dusenberry, distinguishes early on between **ideas** ['valuable though they may be, are a dime-a-dozen in business'] and **insights** ['states a truth that alters how you see the world']. To paraphrase him, a good idea may inspire a great tactic, but a good insight can power a program. Some of my former staff (and a few clients) may recall my interest in centipedes – those insights that suggest a thousand ideas or tactics.

Here's how we developed the creative brief[1] and what follows is the insight that emerged from that process for the National Cancer Institute's 5 A Day Media Campaign:

Lack of top-of-mind awareness, physical invisibility, and perceived amount of effort and time posed obstacles to the target's very positive intentions and preferences for fruits and vegetables over faster, less nutritious foods. The target audience was very much driven by a perceived scarcity of time. The team set the following action: Add two servings of fruits and vegetables 'the easy way instead of the hard way.'

Now the power of this insight isn't that it is worthy of a Nobel Prize, it is what it suggests or implicates as the actions to pursue in all of our marketing and communication efforts. With 5 A Day, it was no longer about 'eat your five servings of fruits and vegetables a day,' a message that we already knew was DOA with our target audience. Instead, our insight led us to focus on 'adding two in easy ways' that immediately prompted attention (the audience did have laudable aspirations to want to eat more healthy), provided suggested actions in a context that were relevant for the audience (making it tangible and easy), and were 'achievable' – or as the behavioral change theorist might put it, they had a high degree of confidence (or self-efficacy) that they could do what was suggested to them.

Phil is, as a creative director, an eager consumer of audience research – as are most good CDs I've known. The problem is what kind of research they're looking for. As you might have guessed, it doesn't involve a single mean, median or mode.

...the only research that matters to me (and to most creative people) is the research that inspires ideas and leads to insights. And the research that consistently delivers insights is the research that lets consumers air out their problems.

It is along this theme, that most audience research is too contrived, focused on the wrong questions, overly choreographed and dispassionately analyzed that Jon, Phil, and I agree. I have literally had clients look over the table at me, say 'I know we shouldn't do this, but...' and then proceed to tally the responses to questions in a focus group — embracing those comfortable means, modes and medians instead of panning for the nuggets of truth and insight that come out of the mouths of the audience. Insight means getting closer to your audience; developing an empathy with them and not hiding behind numbers. As a professional photographer counsels people in taking better pictures: First thing, GET CLOSER!

...so much of what poses for research is little more than people seeking information that confirms their biases, their goals, their inclinations, and their decisions. It has nothing to do with acquiring new information. In a sense this is another form of 'satisfaction research'; it only tells you what you're doing right. This is not how great insights materialize. Insights come from owning up to what you're doing wrong and addressing those problems in ways that matter.

There are many other insights and stories in this book that make it worthwhile. Let's leave with his 'criteria for work that wouldn't get out the door,' or what I suggest program planners use as their 'program plans that won't leave this office.'

- It's dull, boring and unexciting (it doesn't answer for the audience the 'why should I pay attention or care' question).
- It's not differentiating (how does the behavior stand out from what they already do or have been told before to do?).
- It sounds, feels, or looks familiar (where's the originality that will break through both the clutter and their filters?).
- It's off strategy (how does it relate to the insight?).
- It's reaching too hard (it's not relevant to the audience's daily life).
- It's too expensive to do (yes, even the ad agencies think about it!).
- It's offensive, tasteless (add your own political correctness templates).

- It's not just a joke ("That's a one-trick pony – a good idea for one spot but minus the legs to survive as a three year campaign." Being engaging and entertaining and being funny are not necessarily the same thing – just ask your local gamer).
- It's poorly executed (the tactics are just not well thought out).

The most dangerous work of all, though, is ... the one that meets all my criteria. It's dangerous because all those superior attributes might mask the fact that you are opting for cleverness at the expense of human connection.

Note

1. Sutton, S.M., Balch, G.I., Lefebvre, R.C. Strategic questions for consumer-based health communications. *Public Health Reports*, 995;**1**10:725–733.

Behavior Evangelists

A lot is being written about evangelists these days, and I'm not speaking about the ones of the religious persuasion. [Fun Fact: I was actively dissuaded from using the term 'evangelist' in a talk I recently did at the Centers for Disease Control and Prevention. PC you know.] Rather, it is the brand evangelist that has captured the rhetoric, and few have done it better than the folks at Church of the Customer Blog[1].

I was reading yet another article/post about brand evangelists, this time a very good one by Mack Collier at MarketingProfs[2]. His action steps provide a framework for how social marketers can think about our own types of evangelists: what I term behavioral evangelists (now you see where that can go at CDC). The idea behind behavioral evangelists is quite simple: take people who already practice the behaviors you are encouraging, or who quickly adopt them (aka early adopters) - or use the product or service you are marketing - and provide them with the tools and encouragement to 'take the message' to others. This evangelism might be straight word-of-mouth, passing out literature and other materials, sending digital messages to friends through email or SMS, and even volunteering to act as peer counselors or other program disseminators and extenders[3]. Here are the action steps Mack suggests in his article with my own commentary in applying it to a social marketing program.

1. **Make brand evangelism a part of your company from the top down.** Whatever your organization's mission is, discover how your colleagues and co-workers get excited and passionate about their work and fuel it. I can always tell, and so can you, when an organization is successful by the energy you get from the employees; so do your clients and customers. When you feel it, they feel it, and vice versa. It doesn't always have to come through as unbridled enthusiasm either; determination, commitment, compassion are other infectious agents for evangelism - just as brooding, passivity and negativity suck the oxygen right out of the room. When you are excited about the behaviors and changes you are encouraging, it's difficult for others to not catch the spirit as well. Do the attitude check before you go out the door every morning (or as a friend says: bring your A game[4]).

2. **Figure out who your evangelists are and also what common traits they possess.** Understand what it is about the behaviors, products and services you encourage that motivates and is reinforcing to your audience to try

them and evangelize them to other people. An even better idea: find your <u>positive deviants</u>[5] and learn who are your existing evangelists and why they are already doing the desired behaviors and promoting them to others.

3. **Shift your marketing mindset regarding your evangelists to that of a marketing partner.** Your evangelists are your direct link to your target market, and they will happily teach you exactly how to reach them. Find ways to incorporate their feedback into your marketing processes, and give them a greater say into the direction of your program.

4. **Look for ways to put your brand on the same level with your customers.** Make your behavior change programs, your products and your services transparent to your clients. You aren't trying to trick them or deceive them into doing something they really don't want to do (are you?). So open up, let them be part of your process - from beginning to end. Talk with them, often and where they gather, whether it is a social network site or blog, a beauty parlor or a pool hall. Conversations allow you to establish deeper and more meaningful relationships with your priority audiences; the kinds that lead to the <u>world changing insights for your programs</u> and nurture their evangelism.

5. **Create and maintain as many channels of communication as possible between your and your customers.** How many ways can you provide opportunities to talk with your audience, and for them to talk with you? Do more! Mack suggests adding areas on your Web site and blog where customers can leave feedback, including suggestions. Make sure your product packaging includes information on how to contact customer service, and how to leave suggestions and feedback. Put suggestion boxes in the waiting area.

6. **Make it as easy as possible for them to give you feedback.** Add contact forms or email links to your Web site and blog, and include contact information on your product's packaging and any emails you send. And acknowledge receipt of the feedback. Then do something about it and let them know you listened.

7. **View your evangelists as volunteer salespeople for your brand, because that's exactly what they are.** Give them all the information and tools they need to promote your program, behaviors, products and services to their relatives, friends and co-workers. Create an outreach program just for them. Treat them like staff. Make it as easy as possible for your evangelists to promote your program offerings to everyone they come in contact with.

8. **Make every effort to create a sense of community among your evangelists.** We need to make it as easy as possible for our evangelists to come

together and share information, their love of our program and what it does to improve their lives. Our organizations also need to make every effort to be a member of these communities, wherever they occur - and let them run themselves.

Whether you want to call them ambassadors, diffusion agents, volunteer, advocates or evangelists, the logic (and evidence base) for the strategy is clear:

- *Reaching through people is the best way to reach people.*
- *People trust and are most receptive to messages that come from others like them.*
- *Interpersonal communication is the most effective method for behavior change.*
- *Social support enhances maintenance of change.*
- *Advocacy for behavior change also supports one's long term practice of the behavior as well.*

Notes
1. http://customerevangelists.typepad.com
2. http://www.marketingprofs.com
3. Roncarati, DD, Lefebvre, RC, and Carleton, RA.(1989). Voluntary involvement in community health promotion: the Pawtucket Heart Health Program. Health Promotion International, Vol. 4, No. 1, 11-18.
4. http://www.urbandictionary.com/define
5. http://www.positivedeviance.org

Making Citizen Empowerment a Cornerstone

A report from the UK Cabinet (*Excellence and fairness: Achieving world class public services*[1]) charts a new course for reform of, and to achieve excellence in, providing public services in the UK. The vision is based upon three principles: citizen empowerment, a new professionalism in the public workforce and strategic leadership from government. For me, the timing is useful as one context for shaping the US public health objectives for the next decade. For readers who aren't familiar with Healthy People, it is the US government's vehicle for developing, adopting and then acting on public health priorities for the next decade. You can go here for an <u>overview of the Healthy People 2020 process</u>[2] or to the <u>Healthy People 2010 objectives</u>[3] to get an idea of their scope.

The section on citizen empowerment is useful to those of us who are social marketers and claim an audience-centric approach as one of our guiding principles (so do they!). Citizen empowerment is also a core feature for those who see social media and mobile technologies as enabling philosophies and tools. Below are some excerpts from the report that may inspire both your imagination and intention to become involved in opportunities to contribute to national policy development. I'll note here that the original document concerns ALL public services and not just health, though these are the focus of what I extracted. The promises of social marketing and applications of new media are not restricted to just health issues!

<u>Here is the nut of their approach</u>: *The best systems in the world treat each citizen as a unique individual, with his or her own family's distinct needs, and then tailor the service to meet these personalised requirements. No centrally driven or centrally accountable system can operate in this fine-grained way...*

"The underlying quality of public services is better than ever before. The challenge now is to ensure the development of more personalised and responsive, as well as fair and equitable services. Alongside the extension of choice in health and other services, **there must be a deepening of user involvement** through new forms of individual and community control. The exact mechanism will vary from service to service, but the aspiration will be the same: **enabling more personalised services by giving citizens the information and power to shape services around their needs and aspirations, rather than by assuming that someone in the Government knows best."** (my emphasis throughout)

Some of their recommendations to empower citizens include:

*For many services, empowerment starts when people are able to make real choices about which services are best suited to them – their lifestyles and their needs. **Enhancing and extending the opportunities people have to make choices empowers citizens.** It also creates pressure for improvement by rewarding services that offer what people want...in a range of sectors from child-care to primary health, alternative education, probation and employment services.*

"The whole agenda of reform will rest on improved transparency of information about public services and their performance, as well as transparency about the standards that citizens should be able to expect. Effective empowerment rests on good information...Central government is therefore committed to ensuring that, as a matter of course, public services make non-personal information available for re-use. This will include the provision of frequent, comparative and tailored performance data about services at a local level.

"In addition to encouraging collaboration between service users and professionals, **networks of users can also provide personalised and ongoing support to an extent which would be impossible if provided by professionals alone.** For example, the Expert Patients Programme in the UK enables people with personal experience of managing long term conditions to share their knowledge and expertise with others. [Ed Note: and here's <u>a social network site 'specifically designed for organizing helpers</u>[4], where everyone can pitch in with meals delivery, rides, and other tasks necessary for life to run smoothly during times of medical crisis, end-of-life caring, or family caregiver exhaustion.' Just a thought...]

*The Government will therefore extend opportunities for people to become directly involved in making decisions about the treatment and service they receive – the parent, student, patient, tenant or victim of crime becoming a genuine partner in deciding on the best approach. Parents, for example, will be able to influence and support the education of their children through regular interaction with their school via email and text message, as well as regular parents' meetings and reports...The internet has given a powerful voice to consumers to give feedback on private sector services – that feedback is now spreading to public services and must be embraced. <u>NHS</u> Choices[5] is a large scale example of the public sector soliciting feedback on health care, building on the example of websites such as patientopinion.com[6]. **The challenge for public service providers is to listen to and work with websites that provide a rich seam of feedback, even if that feedback makes for uncomfortable reading.***

A deeper form of user engagement involves transferring control of resources to the service user. For example, individual budgets in social care have shown that when people are given control over the funds to be spent on them, they often make changes that significantly improve the care they receive: bringing support closer to home; fitting services more closely around the needs and resources of their family; and getting better value for money in the services they buy.
And the finale -

As the Government seeks to move the public services forward, the next stage of our reform programme must **put power directly into the hands of citizens, driving services to become more responsive and personalised to each individual's needs and aspirations – and provide a strong set of incentives for the system to innovate and improve.** As a consequence:

- *Services should reflect people's aspirations and lifestyles to offer users the increased personal control they demand, and adapt to meet new demands such as more flexible opening hours or better online access.*
- *Services must be designed around people's complex and interrelated needs, for instance providing those with long term health conditions with greater continuity of care between their home and hospital.*
- *A stronger relationship needs to be created between the citizen and public service professionals. Only when citizens are treated as equal partners do they bring their knowledge, time and energy to address challenges such as preventing ill-health.*

Tips for the Lotsa Helping Hands site to Joe Starinchak and for the Cabinet Report to Alan Moore.

Notes
1. http://www.cabinetoffice.gov.uk/strategy/publications/world_class_public_services.pdf.ashx.
2. http://www.healthypeople.gov/HP2020/
3. http://www.healthypeople.gov/Document/html/uih/uih_2.htm#obj
4. http://www.lotsahelpinghands.com/
5. http://www.nhs.uk/Pages/homepage
6. http://www.patientopinion.org.uk

The Audience as Producer

Marketing and communications activities are under significant stress these days. The fragmentation of familiar media to serve niche markets (how many television channels are available, magazine titles are increasing), the proliferation of new ones (social networks sites, mobile) and economics are part of the issue. However, I think the bigger issue for health communication and social marketing is the changing role of the consumer, something I spoke about at the 2007 *Innovation in Social Marketing Conference*. The nut of my argument is that our traditional (and outdated) view of communication as being a linear Source – Message – Channel – Receiver (SMCR) process has been permanently altered, not just in theory, but by Web 2.0 practice and recent research that focuses us on social networks and the principles of engagement, interactivity and media multiplexity[1].

What is under-appreciated by many social marketers who are beginning to experiment with these new technologies is that they are simply not new types of media with which to do the same old things. These new media signal a shift in thinking about how we communicate with our audiences. Even more alarming in using these new media many marketers - commercial and social - continue to perpetuate the myth of the source-message-channel- receiver paradigm rather than embrace the collaborative and dynamic communication models these new technologies embody. While the reality has not changed, what these new technologies make plain is that it is, indeed, a networked world — one in which we do not design 'messages' for priority audiences, stakeholders, partners, donors and others groups, but a world in which they talk back to us, and as importantly, with each other.

When we focus on new media as a tool, rather than a philosophy and approach we have with people formerly known as the audience, we miss the transformative power of the technology. *These new technologies [also] have implications for how we think about the behaviors, products and services we market; the incentives and costs we focus on; and the opportunities we present and places where we interact with our audience and allow them to try new things.*

What some social marketers are getting in all of this is the shifting of audience roles from the consumers of health information and messages to the producers (or at least co-producers for the recovering control freaks) of this information. Another POV on this issue uses the term prosumers[3] - people who alternate being producers and consumers of information, products and services.

Though these shifts in thinking are more enlightened in some ways, they are still missing what I think is the bigger point here: If we are to have successful AND sustainable social marketing programs, we need to focus a larger part of our efforts on encouraging and supporting people to be better producers - period.

Mechai Verivadya, a champion of social marketing approaches to family planning and HIV prevention in Thailand, stated the case in *Health Affairs*[4]:

Many organizations in the developing world - admirable organizations - do excellent work providing health care. Some give it away free. Some sell socially marketed health products. They are all trying to solve health problems that are the consequence of poverty, but they don't address the root cause of poverty. Hence, they will never be sustainable. Once they stop providing free health care, the good health care stops. As for those who sell health care services or products, be it malaria bed nets, contraceptives, or oral dehydration solutions, they are basically serving the upper end of the poor, leaving the poorest unserved.

Why can't we do two things? First, continue to provide free or low-cost health care, medications, and so on, but also have a program for those who are poor and can't afford to buy these health products. Help them engage in business, become barefoot entrepreneurs, and earn a profit so that they can spend some of that profit on health care. This approach enables those who can't afford it to pay for their health care, and that's the difference. It becomes sustainable.

Many social entrepreneurial ventures focus on the same issue: how to assist people to become income producers through socially responsive business activities. A rise in income level through participation in these businesses helps 'the audience' lift themselves, their families and their villages and neighborhoods out of poverty and afford health promotion and health care products and services. Muhammad Yunus also talks about the need for social businesses[5] that focus as much on transforming the formerly passive consumer audience into an active producer one. One of the shortcomings of the Base of the Pyramid[6] (BOP) is that it focuses on the old consumer model rather than giving equal weight to the producer. The BOP Protocol[7] is one attempt to align corporate and local interests in developing business models that emphasize co-creation.

When you consider that we are all marketers, the fact that we pay so little attention to the other role people have in market exchanges - production - is pretty remarkable. Why not use our social marketing knowledge and abilities to use social marketing to address the alleviation of poverty (see the new definition[8]) - a consistently pointed to social determinant of health status[9] around the world?

Notes

1. Lefebvre, R.C. The new technology: The consumer as participant rather than target audience. *Social Marketing Quarterly*, 2007;**13**:31-42.
2. http://en.wikipedia.org/wiki/Prosumer
3. Melnick, G.A. From family planning to HIV/AIDS prevention to poverty alleviation: A conversation with Mechai Viravaidya. *Health Affairs*, 2007;**26**:w670-677 (Published online 25 September 2007 doi: 10.1377/hlthaff.26.6.w670)
4. Yunus, Muhammad. *Creating a World Without Poverty: Social Business and the Future of Capitalism*. Public Affairs™: Perseus Books Group 2008.
5. http://www.nextbillion.net/blog/2008/08/26/reviewing-a-new-bop-critique-published-in-innovations-journal
6. http://www.bop-protocol.org/
7. http://blogs.cgdev.org/globaldevelopment/2008/07/world-bank-revisits-the-meanin.php
8. http://www.who.int/social_determinants/en/

Into the Jungle

Virtual Anthropology

The latest issue of Trendwatching.com's newsletter is devoted to "Virtual Anthropology."[1] Here's how they describe it:

Let's face it, the art of trend watching often isn't particularly academic. A mix of curiosity and open-mindedness, and a fascination with manifestations of the (seemingly) new will get you a long way.

And subsequently applying your findings and spottings and turning them into new goods, services and experiences for, or even better, with your customers is more about creativity and guts than about endless studies and number crunching. Sure, numbers are important, but more as evidence than as a starting point.

No wonder, then, that 'observing' and 'inspiration' are at the core of what trend watchers do, and that many of their activities could be described as a 'diet' (or in Europe: 'light') version of anthropology. To refresh your memory, anthropology consists of the study of mankind with a strong emphasis on fieldwork. To quote Saatchi & Saatchi honcho Kevin Roberts: "If you want to understand how a lion hunts, don't go to the zoo. Go to the jungle."

Their point is that the Generation C trend, among others, is providing millions of opportunities to practice this new art - whether it be through sorting through on-line photo, homemade video or webcam sites; reviewing blogs and online journals; or just looking for ideas by people watching or window shopping in some of the world's most inspirational cities.

In social marketing, we often talk about creating behavior and social change programs that are relevant to our audience's life, yet often all we know about these "lives" are a few demographic and epidemiological statistics, fragments of conversations from a few focus groups, and results of previous research studies. I have been a proponent of introducing more anthropological thinking and techniques into how social marketing conceives formative research studies. This newsletter extends the boundaries for how we can learn more about our lions, lionesses and cubs.

BTW - the article comes complete with multiple links to get your virtual anthropology studies started.

Note
1. http://www.trendwatching.com

Transformative Consumer Research and "At Risk" Populations

What insights, opportunities and projects does transformative consumer research[1] offer people and organizations who work to improve the lives of people identified as being in an 'at risk' group[2]? That was the assignment for our small group that met at the Second Annual Transformative Research Conference. Our discussion group was one of nine convened to create an agenda for the field that will continue in ongoing intellectual exchange, research collaborations, and/or projects aimed at social change.

Our group began by working through the many different types of determinants and moderating variables that are used to traditionally define 'at risk' - among them genetic susceptibilities; social determinants; socio-demographic characteristics; cognitive, emotional and physical (CEP) handicaps; and behaviors. We soon realized that we could spend the day (and even longer) on this descriptive exercise - one that has been ably addressed by many others including the WHO Commission on Social Determinants.[3] What, we asked, is the unique contribution that consumer research and marketing can make towards understanding the concept of 'at risk?'

A definition of an 'at-risk' population, from a marketer's POV, that we roughed out is: *someone who has a personal or situational disadvantage in the marketplace that might create negative outcomes for the individual or society*. It is a draft idea at this point, and will need more discussion and refinement. However, putting 'at risk' in the context of the marketplace - and here marketplace is a broad space and not restricted to shopping and financial transactions - offers social marketers a starting point for what we (should) do best: conduct market analysis to uncover what forces in the marketplace potentiate[4] the impact of personal factors (genetic, biological, CEP handicaps, risky behaviors) and situational ones (poverty, housing, transportation, life stressors, environmental disasters) and how market forces - including changes in the product, service and behavioral choices that are available; their accessibility; the incentive structures and rewards; and how they are communicated to people - can be harnessed to mitigate or even eliminate their impact. (See: *Making Change Happen: The Marketing Approach*)

Throughout the day, our discussion ranged over a number of ideas and approaches to thinking about and serving 'at risk' groups. At one point we stopped to identify some of the tensions emerging in our conversation. The point of this list is not to decide which is necessarily 'right' or 'wrong,' but to offer you what a few consumer researchers and social marketers see as important issues to address when working with these populations:

1. Framing people in these groups as 'vulnerable' versus possessing unique strengths and assets.

2. Focusing on the characteristics of 'typical' people (i.e., how do we work towards inclusion?)[5] versus the uniqueness of people identified as being 'at risk.'

3. Planning for marginal changes in their status (or what was referred to as a corporate model) versus seeking radical changes that are fostered by grassroots activities.

4. Using targeting to focus marketing and other resources versus protecting these groups from it (think about minority population groups and their resistance to targeting by tobacco and alcohol advertisers, other groups who shun being targeted by public health programs because it may lead to further marginalization and stigma).

5. Thinking about people in these groups as being unaware or naive of their elevated risk status (with an accompanying sense of calm) versus stimulating them into action (with the attendant sense of worry and/or fear - is this where people who question when to use fear-based communications need to think a bit longer and harder about what they are doing?).

The challenge for our group, and the others, was to develop several ideas for research projects or programs that could be used to create a transformative consumer research agenda. Our suggestions, that I am sure will be massaged many more times and adapted, are:

1. Conduct a sociological or historical analysis of consumer movements by 'at risk' groups that resulted in positive effects on the marketing practices of corporations and brands. We are especially interested in how a subset of these movements changed the marketers' perception of them as being marginalized (for example, they did not talk about the problem, develop offerings specifically for them, or use models in their ads like them) to being included in the range

of target audiences they serve (for example, the emergence of the gay market, people with CEP handicaps, seniors).

2. How to design decision-making environments that lead to better outcomes in at-risk situations, such as how to display foods in cafeteria lines that lead to lower caloric trays at the cashier or providing health insurance and health care information to different consumer groups.

3. Conduct consumer studies of at-risk groups to understand how to create an ideal consumer space that can then be used by change agents to inform and guide corporate, government, NGO and community actions to achieve them.

4. Studies on how social networks and new information and communications technologies are creating or affecting at-risk populations, for example, by their influence on information processing abilities and skills.

5. Studies on whether there are shared motivational drivers for risky behaviors that may need to be considered in designing programs to address them to avoid unintended effects such as substitution or adoption of other addictive behaviors.

Notes
1. http://www.acrwebsite.org/
2. http://medical-dictionary.thefreedictionary.com/high-risk+group
3. http://www.who.int/social_determinants/thecommission/finalreport/en/index.html
4. http://www.thefreedictionary.com/potentiate
5. http://en.wikipedia.org/wiki/Inclusive_development

Teen Segmentation by Class

danah boyd writes on the division of American teen culture by class[1] as she looks at the differences among users of MySpace and Facebook. She notes that while the use of social class[2] as a construction in other countries (England[3] and India being two examples[4]) is accepted practice, 'class' is not an easy term to apply in American culture and is not the equivalent to socio-economic status[5].

Class divisions in the United States have more to do with social networks (the real ones, not FB/MS), social capital, cultural capital, and attitudes than income...

The goodie two shoes, jocks, athletes, or other "good" kids are now going to Facebook. These kids tend to come from families who emphasize education and going to college. They are part of what we'd call hegemonic society. They are primarily white, but not exclusively. They are in honors classes, looking forward to the prom, and live in a world dictated by after school activities.

MySpace is still home for Latino/Hispanic teens, immigrant teens, "burnouts," "alternative kids," "art fags," punks, emos, goths, gangstas, queer kids, and other kids who didn't play into the dominant high school popularity paradigm. These are kids whose parents didn't go to college, who are expected to get a job when they finish high school. These are the teens who plan to go into the military immediately after schools. Teens who are really into music or in a band are also on MySpace. MySpace has most of the kids who are socially ostracized at school because they are geeks, freaks, or queers.

She uses this self-segregation, or social aggregation (it's your POV), to make the point that the technology allows these social gaps to become clearer even as we (as a society, as harbingers of a unified social norm) try to ignore them. When she notes how the military banned use of MySpace by the troops, but protected Facebook from the same treatment, it was case closed for me.

Read her article and ask yourself when you are working with a health issue how often it involves people from varying socio-economic and demographic backgrounds and how often does it REALLY involve differences in class? How much of the fatalism, lack of control and other 'barriers' we perceive among people engaging in risky behaviors is due to racial/ethnic and income level and how much is really a function of underlying class differences? What makes it relatively easy to stigmatize certain behaviors and then make them so resistant to change? And how often are we paying attention to these class attributes when we develop programs with one audience versus another? When we use 'tribes' to describe some groups of teens[6] we are beginning to come to grips with the issue?

But especially in public health the notion of focusing on tribes as priority audiences, and not some epidemiological defined segment of the population, seems to hit a nerve we'd rather leave unexposed - to whose detriment is the question we can discuss more.

As a society, we have strong class divisions and we project these values onto our kids. MySpace and Facebook seem to be showcasing this division quite well. I wonder how often we do it with our social marketing programs?

Sigh: and I wish we had more ethnographers to help us develop the insights to break away from the rationalistic[7], individualistic[8], and reductionist[9] paradigms enshrined by the epidemiologists that, I believe, are among the strait-jackets for doing great social marketing. (See: *Aspiring to Audience Insights – Part A*)

Notes
1. http://www.danah.org/papers/essays/ClassDivisions.html
2. http://en.wikipedia.org/wiki/Social_class
3. http://www.ncbi.nlm.nih.gov/sites/entrez?cmd=Retrieve&db=PubMed&list_uids=1674771&dopt=Citation
4. http://www.thelancet.com/journals/lancet/article/PIIS0140673605711466/abstract
5. http://www.ncbi.nlm.nih.gov/sites/entrez?cmd=Retrieve&db=PubMed&list_uids=9353663&dopt=Citation
6. http://www.sirc.org/publik/talking_not_taking.shtml
7. http://en.wikipedia.org/wiki/Rationalism
8. http://en.wikipedia.org/wiki/Individualism
9. http://en.wikipedia.org/wiki/Reductionistic

The Digital Youth Project: Teen Socialization and the Internet

The Digital Youth Project, funded by the MacArthur Foundation, released their results yesterday. I am finding the coverage by media such as The New York Times and The San Jose Mercury News to be short on detail and long on anecdote [typical headline: *It is OK for kids to be online*]. SO if you want a quick review of what is going on with this research, the bottomline is: most of the popular ideas adults have (oh, and the media that promote them) about teen use of the internet are wrong. The media release[1] from the Foundation notes the significant findings:

There is a generation gap in how youth and adults view the value of online activity.
- Adults tend to be in the dark about what youth are doing online, and often view online activity as risky or an unproductive distraction.
- Youth understand the social value of online activity and are generally highly motivated to participate.

Youth are navigating complex social and technical worlds by participating online.
- Young people are learning basic social and technical skills that they need to fully participate in contemporary society.
- The social worlds that youth are negotiating have new kinds of dynamics, as online socializing is permanent, public, involves managing elaborate networks of friends and acquaintances, and is always on.

Young people are motivated to learn from their peers online.
- The Internet provides new kinds of public spaces for youth to interact and receive feedback from one another.
- Young people respect each other's authority online and are more motivated to learn from each other than from adults.

Most youth are not taking full advantage of the learning opportunities of the Internet.
- Most youth use the Internet socially, but other learning opportunities exist.
- Youth can connect with people in different locations and of different ages who share their interests, making it possible to pursue interests that might not be popular or valued with their local peer groups.
- "Geeked-out" learning opportunities are abundant – subjects like astronomy, creative writing, and foreign languages.

In the 2-page research brief of the study,[2] the authors draw these implications from their work:

Adults should facilitate young people's engagement with digital media. Contrary to adult perceptions, while hanging out online, youth are picking up basic social and technical skills they need to fully participate in contemporary society. Erecting barriers to participation deprives teens of access to these forms of learning.

Given the diversity of digital media, it is problematic to develop a standardized set of benchmarks against which to measure young people's technical and new media literacy. For example, whereas friendship-driven activities center upon peer culture, adult participation is more welcome in interest-driven ones.

In interest-driven participation, adults have an important role to play. Youth using new media often learn from their peers, not teachers or adults. Yet adults can still have tremendous influence in setting learning goals, particularly on the interest-driven side where adult hobbyists function as role models and more experienced peers.

To stay relevant in the 21st century, education institutions need to keep pace with the rapid changes introduced by digital media. Youths' participation in this networked world suggests new ways of thinking about the role of education.

What I see as the main takeaway for social network strategy with this age group is this:

The researchers identified two distinctive categories of teen engagement with digital media: friendship-driven and interest-driven. While friendship-driven participation centered on "hanging out" with existing friends, interest-driven participation involved accessing online information and communities that may not be present in the local peer group.

I find that most organizations that start dreaming about using new media to reach youth focus on the friendship-driven side of the equation - taking an interest in how to 'reach' or 'engage' individuals on social network sites by making pop culture appeals and associations (try to be a friend). The other option that this research clearly points to is focusing on the specialized knowledge networks and hobby groups that have *social objects* around which teens aggregate (a much more important idea for social marketers than simply 'creating more products' that seems to be the new mantra for some. Check here for some thoughtful ideas on new marketing by Hugh MacLeod).[3] The opportunity with these types of networks is that the participation of adults as 'experienced peers,' not experts, is welcomed.

Notes
1. http://www.macfound.org/site/c.lkLXJ8MQKrH/b.4773437/
2. http://www.macfound.org/atf/cf/%7BB0386CE3-8B29-4162-8098-E466FB856794%7D/DML_ETHNOG_2PGR.PDF
3. http://gapingvoid.com/2008/11/09/blue-monster-why-social-objects-are-the-future-of-marketing/

Communication Patterns of the Millennium Generation

An article in Sunday's *New York Times* profiles 'older' members of the Millennium Generation (those born between 1980-2000) to remind advertisers (& social marketers and health communicators) that the choices in using digital media continue to fracture target audiences and present new challenges for capturing their attention ["A Generation Serves Notice: It's a Moving Target"[1]].

Karell Roxas, 24, a senior editor at Gurl.com, begins each day in her Williamsburg, Brooklyn, apartment with a diet of Gmail, Hotmail, work e-mail, NYTimes ("I haven't picked up a print newspaper in forever," she says) and blogs, in that order. She says it is a necessary regimen for maintaining a functional dialogue both at work and in her circle of friends.

The usual pattern of statistics are reviewed for this group, many of which I've posted on before, and include the preference for text messaging over either email or IM for peer2peer communication, and the heavier use of blogs (nearly 80%). One of the interesting aspects of these trends in media usage are the sociological effects - and their implications for advertising and marketing programs:

The preceding generation may have thought that e-mail, newsgroups, Web forums and even online chats accelerated the word-of-mouth phenomenon. They did. But they are nothing compared with the always-live electronic dialogue among millions of teenagers and 20-somethings.

For the millennials "...reliance and trust in nontraditional sources - meaning everyday people, their friends, their networks, the network they've created around them - has a much greater influence on their behaviors than traditional advertising."
Magid calls it the peer-to-group phenomenon - a digital-age manifestation of the grapevine.

"When someone wants to share it, forward it, record it, take a picture of it, whatever the case may be, that puts it into a form of currency," Mr. McKenzie said. "And when marketing gets to a level of currency, then it has achieved nirvana status."

Meaning that the challenge for marketers is how to create peer2group exchanges that feature their brands, products, services and behaviors. The question is no longer "what motivates someone to change" but rather "what motivates someone to share something they find intrinsically useful and valuable with their most trusted friends and colleagues?" And of course: what makes something useful and valuable to them to begin with? We need to become more focused on not just behavior change outcomes for individuals, or environmental and policy changes, but social network changes that guide and support our efforts both up and down the river.

Note
1. http://www.nytimes.com/2006/01/22/business/yourmoney/22youth. html

Segmenting Black Americans

Among the more frustrating things of doing social marketing with the wannabes is their insistence to segment the general population by race and ethnicity - and then leave it at that! 'We have to have a program for African Americans, Hispanics, etc...!' is the rhetoric and practice. Yet, the assumption that these are homogeneous segments (OK, maybe age and gender get factored in at times) is the frustration when it comes to action: we know the assumption isn't reality, but our government surveys don't give us opportunities to understand our audiences as people rather than demographics. Consequently our programs rarely capture the insights of their daily lives (See: *Aspiring to Audience Insights – Part B*) unless the intrepid few have the resources to do some qualitative research.

Radio One, in conjunction with Yankelovich, has recently issued a series of reports and fact sheets that deserve wide attention among social marketers and health communicators. The *Black America Today* study[1] is billed as the largest segmentation study based on a survey of 3,400 African Americans between 13 and 74 years of age. The report identifies 11 segments and the segmentation analysis identifies differences among Black America from what it means to be Black today to consumer trends, media preferences and confidence in key institutions (such as the church, government, financial services companies and the media). Here are the segments with brief descriptors (fuller reports of each one[2]).

Connected Black Teens: They are tech savvy, highly social, brand driven and fans of Black music (Hip Hop and R&B). They have a plan for their future, they want to preserve Black cultural traditions and believe that too much focus is put on the oppression of Blacks.

Digital Networkers: Over half of this web savvy, high tech, mobile segment are college or high school students who 'network' heavily using Facebook, MySpace, instant messaging and their cell phones. They are saving money – to buy a home or for retirement.

Black Onliners: Heavy web users, this mostly male segment is stressed by their work/life balance and the need to straddle Black and White worlds; they are focused on money as the most meaningful measure of success and are the most stressed of any segment about 'having to fit in'. They are the most frequent users of Black websites and the most frequent online shoppers.

Stretched Black Straddlers: Mostly 18-34, this online, cell phone toting segment is the most stressed by 'straddling' the needs of family and work. Stressed about money and a lack of time, they are heavy users of Black TV and websites and the most likely to say they have been racially discriminated against in the past three months.

New Middle Class: The best educated, most employed and wealthiest segment is mostly between the ages of 25 and 44 and is the most technologically forward segment. They are the most likely to describe themselves as Black rather than African-American and to believe that problems in the Black community can best be solved by Blacks. They are positive about the future and forward looking.

Family Struggles: Mostly female and heavy TV watchers, this segment is struggling economically and is stressed trying to raise their children on a tight budget. They are the most likely of any segment to relate to the ways Blacks are portrayed on Black TV. Most of their friends and co-workers are Black.

Black is Better: This confident, optimistic, fun-loving segment is very focused on family and their job. They are the most responsive to Black media and most likely to 'buy Black', consistent with their very strong focus on Black culture, history and solidarity.

Sick and Stressed: Mostly over the age of 35, this struggling segment is stressed about money and health, pessimistic about their personal future, and least likely to say things are getting better for them. They are the least likely to have a healthy lifestyle, to play sports or work out or have health insurance.

Faith Fulfills: This highly religious segment, who spend more time than average volunteering for religious or non-profit organizations, is most likely to trust God to take care of things. With an average age of 48, they experience low levels of stress and are the least likely to have been raised by a single parent or to worry about money a lot.

Broadcast Blacks: Highly confident, independent and positive in their attitudes, this female-skewed, older segment is the most likely to say things are getting better for them. They are heavy users of TV and radio (especially Gospel radio) and have the lowest Internet usage. They place high importance on 'buying Black'.

<u>Boomer Blacks:</u> This 'oldest' segment (average 52) is tech savvy with high ownership of computers, DVRs, home theater systems and wireless internet access – 90% are online. They are the most likely to believe that Black children should have Black role models and that it's important to take advantage of the opportunities won by previous generations.

Some of the overall analysis highlights find (each segment has a more complete and targeted analysis):

- 82% said they believe it is "important for parents to prepare their children for prejudice"
- 34% agree that "too much focus is put on the oppression of Blacks"
- Among teens, 52% think there is too much focus on the oppression of Blacks
- More (48%) think that things got better since the Civil Rights struggles of the 60s—than the 1/3 say who say things aren't better
- The majority (76%) have not been discriminated against in the past three months
- African-Americans are more than twice as likely to really trust Black media (30%) as they are to trust mainstream media (13%)

Education and Black media get the highest level of "trust to treat you and your family fairly" at 30%

- The health care system and financial institutions are tied as far as trust at 24% for #2
- Almost everyone—88%—has enormous respect for the opinions and desires of older family members

Media consumption patterns overall include:

- 45 hours a week watching TV, not including time spent watching DVDs
- 84% of households have cable or satellite Media Consumption (Internet)
- Among Blacks age 13-74, 68% are online; Among Black teens, its over 90% that are online
- Spend 31 hours a week using the Internet
- Spend 22 hours listening to AM or FM radio in a typical week

- Nearly 9 in 10 spend more than an hour reading magazines every week
- Spend 2 hours a week reading the newspaper Black Media Consumption

Among all Black households, 81% watch Black TV channels weekly; 66% believe there should be more television shows that focus on Blacks.
Of the TV watched in a typical week, 32% is spent watching channels focused on African Americans/Blacks.

Now if Radio One would get involved with the public health people to help apply this segmentation analysis to health issues, we will have an even more powerful tool. But for now, it's more information than what we have had before about how people cluster in terms of their lives - not their disease status.

Notes
1. http://www.blackamericastudy.com/summary/
2. http://www.blackamericastudy.com/segments/

Hispanic Population Groups and Wireless Broadband Access

A new report by The Hispanic Institute and Mobile Future, "Hispanic Broadband Access: Making the Most of the Mobile, Connected Future," demonstrates the pervasiveness of wireless broadband services in their daily lives.[1] Highlights of the report include:

1. While Hispanics trail other U.S. populations in overall Internet access, they are among the most avid users of mobile broadband. In fact, Hispanics and African Americans lead mobile broadband use (53% and 58% respectively), with both communities far ahead of Whites (33%).

2. Hispanics are more mobile than the general U.S. population and, thus, rely more on cell phones. In fact, compared to Americans generally, Hispanics account for more minutes used and for a higher percentage of cell-phone ownership despite their relatively low incomes.

3. Given that roughly 40% of U.S. Hispanics are born abroad, in countries where wireless service often is more common than landline phones, the American Hispanic community is more open to mobile broadband than many other population groups. This familiarity makes the leap to smartphones and other connected mobile devices a more intuitive step for many than turning to wired, home broadband adoption and computer usage.

4. In 2008, Hispanics outpaced the general population in accessing and downloading digital media (music, video, audio, movies, television programs, video games and podcasts), 42% to 35%.

At the talks I do about social and mobile media, most public health people are stunned to learn that Hispanics are such avid mobile users. Indeed, the first objection to using mobile and SNS is that 'they will not reach my population.' As I say then, and here again, get your preconceptions behind you. Hard-to-reach is a source-driven construct, not an audience-driven one.

Note
1. http://www.thehispanicinstitute.net/node/1820

Health Literacy and Health Care

Why do you cover health literacy in a class on social marketing? An innocent question on one hand, but also one that demonstrates the 'curse of knowledge' that haunts so many people in public health and social change who are oblivious to the insidious nature of health illiteracy. Learning how to promote health behavior and social engagement by communicating the right words at the right times to the right people, re-arranging the physical and social environments to provide more access and opportunities for more personally and socially beneficial behaviors, and removing barriers and increasing incentives to do the right things are all fine. But what if our audiences don't even understand what we are talking about - or can't hum the tune, let alone read the words on the sheet?

That's what should make health literacy an important upstream issue for social marketers. I've talked about the dismal statistics in the US, and now Canadian public health professionals are having their eyes opened to a problem that not only undermines health promotion efforts, but the quality of health care, for decades to come. From the <u>State of Learning in Canada</u> report.[1]

More than half (55%) of Canadians aged 16 to 65 do not have levels of health literacy adequate to read nutrition labels, follow medication directions, understand safety instructions, or make informed and adequate choices for their own healthy living.
Health literacy is particularly low among seniors, who require health services most and are pre-scribed the greatest number of medications. Of all Canadians older than 65, 88% lack the literacy skills needed to deal with health information.

Low educational attainment and health illiteracy are not going to simply disappear as social determinants of health status and health care. Upstream social marketers and consumer advocates need to understand these issues from the people's POV and communicate these effectively to health policymakers who blithely seem to believe that the consumer can and should be in charge of making their own health care decisions - regardless of what they have to say! In fact, there is little evidence for how health literacy may impact the ability of patients to understand and use the basic building blocks of health care reform initiatives such as electronic and personal health records.

Where are the audience-driven research studies with these population groups around these life-or-death and quality-of-life issues? Health care reform is too important to leave just to the experts.

Note
1. http://www.ccl-cca.ca/CCL/Reports/StateofLearning/StateofLearning2007.htm?Language=EN

Few Adults Have Skills to Make Sound Decisions

If you are involved with health promotion and disease prevention programs, health screening programs, health care and patient education or health policy – these data should shock you.

Fewer than 1 in 8 (12%) American adults are proficient in health literacy skills. What this means is that approximately 191 million Americans cannot:

- Calculate an employee's share of health insurance costs for a year, using a table that shows how the employee's monthly cost varies depending on income and family size.
- Find the information required to define a medical term by searching through a complex document.
- Evaluate information to determine which legal document is applicable to a specific health care situation.

Almost half (47%) of adults cannot:

- Determine a healthy weight range for a person of a specified height, based on a graph that relates height and weight to body mass index (BMI).
- Find the age range during which children should receive a particular vaccine, using a chart that shows all the childhood vaccines and the ages children should receive them.
- Determine what time a person can take a prescription medication, based on information on the prescription drug label that relates the timing of medication to eating.
- Identify three substances that may interact with an over-the-counter drug to cause a side effect, using information on the over-the-counter drug label.

These skills all relate to a concept known as health literacy which is defined by the US Department of Health and Human Services[1] and the Institute of Medicine[2] as: *The degree to which individuals have the capacity to obtain, process, and understand basic health information and services needed to make appropriate health decisions.*

The IOM states that health literacy skills are needed for dialogue and discussion, reading health information, interpreting charts, making decisions about participating in research studies, using medical tools for personal or family health care—such as a peak flow meter or thermometer—calculating timing or dosage of medicine, or voting on health or environment issues. Earlier estimates of adults with low literacy skills had placed the figure at about 90 million.

In 2003, for the first time the National Assessment of Adult Literacy (NAAL) also included an assessment of health literacy among a random sample of over 19,000 American adults. This assessment involved having each adult complete tasks designed to measure their ability to handle everyday tasks associated with maintaining their heath and engaging with the health care system. Measures of prose, document and quantitative literacy skills were combined into an overall health literacy score.

Sponsored by the US Department of Education, the health literacy results of this massive household survey were quietly released in September (*The Health Literacy of America's Adults: Results From The 2003 National Assessment of Adult Literacy*[3]) Among some of the other findings from NAAL are:

• Women and men have about the same rates of health literacy proficiency (12% vs 11 %).
• Whites (14%) and Asian/Pacific Islanders (18%) have higher rates than Blacks (2%) or Hispanics (4%).
• Rates of proficiency peak among adults 25-39 years old (16%) and decline to 3% in adults 65 years and older.
• Health literacy is associated with education level, yet only 27% of people with a bachelor's degree are assessed as being proficient.

A 'basic' level of health literacy proficiency is identified by tasks such as being able to give two reasons a person with no symptoms of a specific disease should be tested for the disease, based on information in a clearly written pamphlet.

People with self-rated poor or fair overall health were very likely to have 'below basic' health literacy skills (42% and 33% respectively). That is, they would not be able to perform the above task.

Between 27-30% of all persons with no health insurance or who received Medicaid or Medicare were assessed as having 'below basic' health literacy.

These are sobering statistics in a world where health information is becoming more complex, communication channels are heavily text oriented (37-41% of people with 'below basic' health literacy report getting none of their health information from books, brochures, newspapers or magazines and 80% get no health information from the Internet), and the health care system is placing more burdens and responsibilities on consumers as part of the consumer-directed health care movement[4].

The data should serve as a wake up call for people at all levels of the public health and health care enterprises who believe that a better educated person is a healthier and wiser one. The basic building blocks of health literacy skills are a prerequisite.

I am a member of the Health Communication Working Group for Healthy People 2010[5], and speaking only for myself, these data-based estimates are the first to document the size of the problem of health illiteracy in the US. They clearly point to the need for both broad-based and targeted programs designed to improve health literacy skills among adults.

The results of NAAL also point to an even greater need for attention by health communicators, patient educators, health care providers – indeed, throughout the entire healthcare system from worksite benefits managers to voluntary health organizations to medical researchers, to assess health literacy skills among their audiences and test their forms, education materials and other products (text, audio and video) for comprehension and ease-of-use among all of their client and patient populations.

Assume that all of your audiences and patients have problems with health literacy skills and you will probably be right 9 times out of 10.

Notes
1. http://www.health.gov/communication/literacy/default.htm
2. http://www.iom.edu/en/Reports/2004/Health-Literacy-A-Prescription-to-End-Confusion.aspx
3. http://nces.ed.gov/pubsearch/pubsinfo.asp?pubid=2006483
4. http://content.healthaffairs.org/cgi/content/full/hlthaff.25.w516/DC2
5. http://www.health.gov/communication/healthypeople/default.htm

Massive Passives

It is 'the beginning of the end of television as we know it' declares a study from the IBM Institute for Business Value[1].

Our analysis indicates that market evolution hinges on two key market drivers: openness of access channels and levels of consumer involvement with media. For the next 5-7 years, there will be change on both fronts — but not uniformly. The industry instead will be stamped by consumer bimodality, a coexistence of two types of users with disparate channel requirements. While one consumer segment remains passive in the living room, the other will force radical change in business models in a search for anytime, anywhere content through multiple channels.

What this means for any health communications or social change program that intends to use communication technologies is that you will need to determine how your audience fractures into these segments of media users. Planning will need to include strategies that reach and resonate with this bimodal distribution of media consumers, with consumer control over their media exposure being of the most concern (see the large shift of the Massive Passive segment over the next 5-7 years). The authors of the study also note the importance of providing 'seamless content mobility' across delivery devices to meet the needs of the open access segments.

Note
1. http://www935.ibm.com/services/us/index.wss/ibvstudy/imc/a10231 72?cntxt=a1000062&re=endoftv

Segmenting Parents in Obesity Prevention Programs

The surge of interest in developing social marketing programs for obesity prevention (and reduction) at the community, state and national levels will unleash a lot of creativity, and a lot of "me too," when it comes to defining priority audiences. Hopefully, many program designers will quickly move beyond simple demographics and begin mapping behaviors that are important to the prevention of childhood obesity. When these exercises are done, PARENTS will loom large in people's thinking about potential audiences. Here are two resources to consider when thinking about this group of people.

The report of the Healthy Lifestyles and Disease Prevention Campaign[1] (Small Steps) identifies a group of parents they describe as "Family Builders" - adults 25-49 years old with children under the age of 18 living at home. These Family Builders are a subset of a larger group termed "Jaded Can't Doers" – adult men and women of all races and ethnicities who may or may not be overweight, want to incorporate healthier behaviors into their life, but without drastically changing their lifestyle. They need to be convinced that a healthier lifestyle is indeed possible. The campaign estimates that this segment comprises 36% of the US population. Read more about the campaign and its communication strategies at the Small Step[2] website.

A recent report in Pediatrics[3] by Rhee and colleagues documented that parents of overweight or obese children aged 2 to 12 years could be segmented by stages of change constructs with respect to their readiness to *help their child lose weight* (emphasis added). Though this study did not take the next step of designing specific programs aimed at parents in various stages, it does provide a useful behavioral segmentation variable to consider in thinking about interventions for parents. Note that this latter study focuses on parents as an audience that would be considered "crucial for success" for a social marketing program with the objective of reducing or preventing overweight and obesity among children. In the Small Steps campaign, the priority audience is clearly adults and more specifically those in a 'contemplation' or even 'precontemplation' frame of mind (they are not reported as giving any indication of a motivation to change their behavior within the next six months). While the rationale for targeting Family Builders as the models and reinforcers of healthier behaviors among their children is solid, the incorporation of their own readiness to help their children

(See: *Segmentation: The First Critical Decision - Step 2*) seems to make sense here as a way of potentially increasing the effectiveness of the intervention.

Notes

1. http://www.smallstep.gov/pdf/obesity_whitepaperfinal_71205.pdf
2. http://www.smallstep.gov/
3. Rhee, K.E., Lumeng, J.C., Appugliese, D.P., Kaciroti, N., Bradley, R.H. Parenting styles and overweight status in first grade. *Pediatrics*, 2006; **117**:2047-2054.

Pediatricians Drowning in Advice

We often hear various representatives of the public lamenting yet another health missive or directive to change behaviors to improve or protect their health and well-being. Most often, physicians are identified by both the agencies responsible for disseminating this information - whether government or voluntary sector - and by people as the most authoritative and credible 'source' (let's start calling them for what they are - interpersonal channels) for communicating this information.

And new evidence is in an issue of *Pediatrics* to suggest that the channel is swamped –"Drowning in a Sea of Advice: Pediatricians and American Academy of Pediatrics Policy Statements."[1]

The authors identify 162 separate pieces of verbal advice pediatricians are recommended to provide their patients by policies established by their professional association (forget what the government and voluntary health associations also want them to say!). These 'words of wisdom' include 109 for preventing injuries, 19 about media use and 8 for substance abuse.

The authors conclude: *The expectation that delivery of all of this advice can be achieved is unrealistic. Moreover, none of the reviewed statements were found to include an evidence-based discussion of the efficacy of the suggested advice. In light of these findings, we suggest that committees should consider both the feasibility and the evidence of efficacy of office-based health advice when generating future policy statements.*

Two points here: (a) the channel is swamped, and the knee-jerk tactic of 'have their doctor talk to them about it' is just that. Remember at some point they are also suppose to diagnose and treat presenting complaints and on-going medical conditions; (b) as the authors note, many recommendations for physicians are not evidence-based as to their anticipated effectiveness, but rather are based on the source credibility myth ['if we say it, they will change'].

Good to remember that doctors are audiences too (See: *Improving Physicians Prescribing Behaviors*)!

Note

1. Belamarich, P.F., Gandica, R., Stein, R.E.K., Racine, A.D. Drowning in a sea of advice: Pediatricians and American Academy of Pediatrics policy statements. *Pediatrics*, 2006;**118**:964-978

Segmenting Cell Phone Users

Going mobile should be an audience-driven decision and not a result of some type of technology envy[1]. Some of the questions you need to be asking when considering a mobile campaign[2] as part of your marketing strategy are: who is already using the technology? How are they engaging with it - what kinds of functionalities do they prefer? And a third is: where are the openings? [Not what are my peers, role models, or competitors doing?]

New research by comScore Networks[3] addresses some of these issues. In their national panel survey of cell phone users in the US, they found three age-related segments.

The Cellular Generation: Ages 18 to 24, these young adults grew up with cell phone awareness, experiencing cell phones as a part of their everyday lives.

Transitioners: Ages 25 to 34, these people fall in between two distinct groups: those who grew up with cell phone knowledge and those who did not. Cell phones began to infiltrate everyday life during their teen years and early adulthood.

Adult Adopters: Age 35 or older, this group was not exposed to cell phone until adulthood. Adult Adopters tend to have the most functional view of cell phones, with many requiring just the basics and showing limited interest in emerging technologies.

As for the engagement question, multiple functions rule:

The Cellular Generation clearly places the greatest value on additional features, with 57 percent ranking text messaging of "high importance" when selecting a wireless carrier and 25 percent stating the same for instant messaging, in both cases higher than their more senior counterparts. Forty-two percent of the Cellular Generation said that a camera was of high importance when selecting a wireless phone and 20 percent said the same of an MP3 Player. In comparison, a lower 30 percent of Adult adopters felt that having a camera was of high importance, and just 8 percent felt the same about an MP3 Player.

Wait a minute! 30% of Adult Adopters give high priority to having text messaging and camera features when selecting a cell phone? Shelve that stereotype.

More than three-quarters of both the Cellular Generation and Transitioners have the option to access the Internet on their cell phones, but Transitioners (29 percent) are more likely to subscribe to Internet services than the Cellular Generation (23 percent). Adult adopters have been the slowest to adopt this behavior, with just 13 percent currently subscribing to the Internet on their cell phones while 42 percent either lack, or are unaware of the option of doing so.

And my favorite survey item that gets at engagement or the relationship you have with your cell phone: I like my phone to be personalized. Strongly Agree: 41% of Cellulars, 32% of Transitioners, and 19% of Adult Adopters.

Now the research questions become: When, where, how and in what states-of-mind are these different groups of people open to health and social change uses of their phones? I expect that means further refinements in segmentation schemes. And how do the benefits of these different types of behaviors differ for each of these groups? Michael Mace[4] offers a user segmentation scheme to get closer to possible answers:

Entertainment-focused users who are generally younger than average and see a mobile device as a lifestyle choice. The biggest use is for game-playing and media (music and video), but also social messaging[5] with their friends.

Communication-focused users who want a mobile device that lets them keep up with others in multiple ways including E-mail, SMS, voice, conferencing, and video calling.

Information-centric users who want their mobile device to be a memory supplement and a means to capture new information.

He uses this scheme to focus on markets for mobile devices and argues for differentiation of devices between markets, not convergence to capture them all. The same rationale may also apply in developing social marketing and social engagement programs that appeal to these different types of users. Knowing what types of cell phones and services people use and how they use them are the new 'channel' questions to be asking your priority audiences.

Notes

1. http://news.cnet.com/
2. http://mobileactive.org/
3. http://www.comscore.com/Press_Events/Press_Releases/2007/01/Cell_Phones_and _18-24_Year_Olds
4. http://mobileopportunity.blogspot.com/2007/01/shape-of-smartphone-and-mobile-data.html
5. http://mobilecrunch.com/2006/12/18/mobile-social-communities-to-see-massive-increase-over-next-4-years/.

Policy Maker Audience

"Upstream" interventions, or those aimed at audiences that can influence environmental and policy change, are often a mystery to many social marketers who confront these unique challenges for the first time. Social marketers who work in the policy change arena have had few resources that directly address the interface of policy change and social marketing. Here are a few to get you started.

As early as 1988, Murray & Douglas[1] noted "If our product is to be defined as policy consultation, then it must include an interactive component, a capacity to feed back from the external environment through the policy developer, aspects of the social, economic and political realities which are true for the policymaker." They go on to identify key audiences for this enterprise as being policy makers, media, and the public. Their analysis led them to call for a three step marketing effort: a long term strategy to prepare policy makers, the media and public for policy change; a short-term strategy to take advantage of opportunities to initiate policy change as they arise; and a broad marketing effort to encourage public support for the policy once it has passed into law.

Two more recent studies have looked at the question of how to apply social marketing principles to meet the information needs of policy makers. Sutton & Thompson[2] conducted quantitative research with 29 policy makers. Their findings included:

- Policy makers are overwhelmed by the large quantity of research directed toward them and perceive that it lacks relevant and useful information.
- The research they receive fails to meet their needs because it does not draw differences or provide implications for policy makers that can be used to support different positions.
- Policy makers have confidence in peer-reviewed articles. However the extended timelines (publication lag) and limited accessibility of this research forces them more often to rely on less credible sources of information.
- The inability to access information when they need it often results in policy decisions being made without data.
- The unavailability of timely, accurate data is largely attributable to a system that they say is broken. Some policy makers use their own personal networks (or "informed experts") to close this gap.

The authors conclude that policy research programs must recognize policy makers as a primary audience and research findings should be designed as a product or service to meet their needs using social marketing principles.

Sorian & Baugh[3] conducted interviews with 292 state government legislators and legislative staff. Among their findings was that 35% of the policy-related material the respondents received are never read: a result that is in part determined by the timeliness and relevance of the information to current policy debates. Legislative staffs are more likely to read the details of policy reports while the legislators are more interested in one-two page briefs with short, bulleted paragraphs. Nearly 84% of policy makers report preferences for trusted sources of information such as a professional association, a state group, a foundation, or a State or Federal Government agency. And while the debates flourish among policy researchers about discussing the implications of the research, 89% of the respondents indicated a desire to know how the researcher views the implications and wants to see/hear their recommendations even if they do not ultimately follow that advice. Finally, survey participants felt overwhelmed by the amount of information they receive, and expressed an interest in ways to identify research and key experts in specific fields. The key takeaway messages for the authors of this study were: policymakers should not be underestimated in their ability to understand the strengths and limitations of research. Timeliness and relevance to current debates is a key factor in policy makers' and shapers' attentiveness to policy research. And finally, these audiences have different information needs and communication preferences that need to be addressed by social marketing program designers and implementers.

Notes

1. Murray, G.G., Douglas, R.R. Social marketing in the alcohol policy arena. *British Journal of Addiction*, 1988; **83**:505-511.
2. Sutton, S., Thompson, E. An in-depth interview study of health care policy professionals and their research needs. *Social Marketing Quarterly*, 2001;7:16-26
3. Sorian, R., Baugh, T. Power of information: Closing the gap between research and policy. *Health Affairs*, 2002;**21**:262-273.

Doing Quality Market Research

Mention doing research for a social marketing project and the reactions are usually of three kinds:

- The 'eye-rollers' who wonder (out loud and in the halls) how much time and budget the activity will drain away from 'the important work.'
- The 'spinning wheels' who immediately launch into dissertations about the strengths and weaknesses of various methodologies and experimental designs that could be employed - and the 1,000+ questions that could be asked!
- The 'glassy stares' who immediately recount their experience with a basic statistics class and swear to have forgotten what a correlation means.

It may seem amusing at first, but 90% of reactions in ALL meetings I have ever been in where the 'R option' is brought up fall into these three categories. It is the primary reason most public health and social change projects fail to reach their lofty objectives: most research is either avoided or designed to confirm the known - and baffle the rest of us. Why are there so few 'bright eyes' (that other 10%) who light up at the opportunity for discovery?

Jacob Nielsen, who is one of the gurus in the usability testing business, was recently writing about Fast, Cheap and Good[1] (pick any two) research. He makes an exceptional point that I have adopted as my own:

The quality criterion for market research is that it changes the world. By this I mean not the literal, but the practical implications the research findings have for the work and the way the team views it (and there is nothing so telling in this respect as when the 'eye-rollers' get briefed on the results, their eyes light up and you see the ideas start to form).

World-changing research sets a direction for the program, often one that nobody expected at the beginning. It brings actionable ideas for how to develop and implement important aspects of the project. And it provides not just new insights into our audiences, (See: *Aspiring to Audience Insights — Part B*) but brings a depth to these insights that drives a strong strategy (what I refer to as *centipedes* - one with many legs).

Here's a simple (and cheap) example. We were asked to design a project to help reduce the incidence of statutory rape. A full day briefing by experts from the health department, epidemiologists, lawyers, police, school administrators and others all went down the same track: tell these perpetrators to STOP IT or ELSE.

Well, as a marketer the enforcement approach isn't my first option (See: *Now That's Cheating*). So with no research budget, we went to one of the places with a higher reported incidence of statutory rapes (a seaside town popular with high school and college students on weekends) and asked around with men what was going on. The response was world changing: *The way some of them get dressed up and get served [liquor] in the bars, who thinks about them being underage?*

Now if you want to be a cynic - fine. Or you can develop a program that wound up featured in national press coverage[2] and generated plenty of buzz.

No, the campaign itself didn't end statutory rape or change the world. But it did present a way for people to think and talk about a problem[3] that was not often raised in public. And it started with a research-based insight that was world changing for the people responsible for the campaign.

Notes
1. http://www.useit.com/alertbox/fast-methods.html
2. http://www.foxnews.com/story/0,2933,129122,00.html
3. http://www.washingtonpost.com/wp-dyn/articles/A41683-2004Jun14. html

The Marketing Blender

Social Marketing and Tobacco Control Policy

"We don't sell guns everywhere, we don't sell alcohol everywhere and we don't need to be selling tobacco everywhere. They're all dangerous products, and they all require regulation."

That is Barbara Ferrer, director of the Boston Public Health Commission, in a story by Katie Zazima in the Sunday *New York Times* about a proposed ban on the sale of cigarettes in drugstores and on college campuses, as well as the closing of the city's cigar and hookah clubs.[1] For me, it is reminder that when we talk about applying social marketing to social problems, and not just individual ones, we should be thinking broadly. And for the Boston Public Health Commission, they need to be thinking broadly as well.

One of the more neglected areas of social marketing is this intersection with public policy. Mike Rothschild, for example, has drawn a line between marketing and regulation, arguing that marketing stops where policy and regulation begin.[2] Others like Stephen Dann, and at times myself, have decried the knee-jerk reaction to fashion regulation to govern individual behaviors before attempting to use other social marketing tools (and here is maybe where I diverge, and now digress).

In the evolution of tobacco control efforts, public health advocates began shifting their strategies from communications (or *1P marketing*) - award-winning public service announcements, well-covered publicity events, evocative posters and culturally appropriate pamphlets - to a broader consideration of the marketing mix. Few of them would have framed it as such at the time. This began with the realization that communications were not getting it done in the COMMIT study (at that time, many people wondered why the groups of investigators responsible for the large community-based CVD prevention studies did not become involved in that multi-community study. The answer was simple: we knew tackling smoking cessation among heavy smokers was going to take more than communication campaigns). As the COMMIT project went on, the idea of media advocacy came front and center - use the media not for education, but to set an agenda for large-scale change by calling attention to the social and environmental determinants of the initiation, maintenance and cessation of smoking behaviors (stop blaming the victim).

The COMMIT study led to the even larger ASSIST project, a 17 state initiative that focused on policy change to support tobacco control efforts. It was early in that project that Mike Pertschuk, a collaborator in the ASSIST Coordinating Center who led the efforts of the Advocacy Institute to support this project, and myself, were called in to the National Cancer Institute offices to reconcile the media advocacy approach (which he represented) and the social marketing approach (that was me) as the intervention model was being debated and developed. They literally had us sit at opposite ends of a very long table and staff crowded into the room: the show down between opposite views of the world.

In fact, though Mike did try and throw the black hat on social marketing (we focus on individual level change and blame victims), by the end of the hour we had complete agreement on the basics. Tobacco control needed to focus on upstream issues (in one vernacular) or the other 4Ps in another. Product features, including on package labeling, the development of brands targeted at specific (and often vulnerable) groups of people, were fair game. Pricing, particularly increasing the price of cigarettes through increases in excise taxes was another. Enacting and enforcing laws to reduce the availability of cigarettes by not selling them to minors and reducing the opportunities to smoke through workplace smoking and health policies became core outcomes. And using communications to set the public agenda and develop support for policy initiatives at the local level, focus on policy-makers as a key audience and devote resources on prevention programs aimed at youth (not one OR the other, but all three) rounded out the model. Mike had his complete advocacy agenda met, and I had a complete social marketing program strategy set. Even before then, and this was 1992, the idea that advocacy and social marketing are mutually exclusive ways of looking at the world had eluded me, but then I grew up applying social marketing for large-scale change in communities, not individual behavior change. What media advocacy and social marketing do together is provide a broader framework for thinking about the context and determinants of behaviors among groups of people (a public health perspective), identify the leverage points through a marketing analysis focused on the 4Ps, and then focus on the audiences that are critical for success (public opinion leaders, media gatekeepers, elected officials).

ASSIST achieved startling successes in some states, and overall made a modest contribution to reducing tobacco use in those states and in the US in general. A great deal of attention throughout the project was also spent of dissemination and diffusion. With the Advocacy Institute's SCARCNet electronic communication system (a few readers may remember fondly), an email, list serve and bulletin board created a national and global community that could share ideas, brainstorm responses to tobacco industry attacks and new marketing strategies and learn from each other. This forerunner of our current social network sites, solidified what has become a paragon of public health (large scale) intervention models.

Returning to Boston, the old approach of regulation as a top-down model also has much to learn from ASSIST and similar projects. For any public policy initiative a marketing approach is a valuable ally. It can not only help identify the most important issues to focus on (products, services and behaviors; prices; distribution, opportunities and access) but it also puts on equal footing how the communication effort needs to drive and sustain public support for these initiatives while also focusing on narrower segments of the population (in this case, business owners) to create a win-win scenario for them as well.

<u>Social change, unlike economics and game theory, does not have to be a zero-sum game.</u> **Social marketing is not the public relations function of public policy; when done well, it becomes the integrator and strategic driver of the entire process with a focus determined from the consumer-perspective and aimed at empowering them.**

Notes
1. http://www.nytimes.com/2008/10/26/us/26smoking.html?_r=1&th&emc=th
2. Rothschild, M.L. Carrots, sticks, and promises: A conceptual framework for the management of public health and social issue behaviors. *Journal of Marketing*, 1999;**63**;24-37.
3. http://cancercontrol.cancer.gov/tcrb/monographs/6/index.html
4. http://www.cancer.gov/newscenter/assistQandA

Be Like Reynolds Wrap

Being a social marketer, I have dreamed of having the HUGE media budgets, DAZZLING creative and MASSIVE distribution systems of such brands as Coke, Pepsi and McDonald's. Who wouldn't want their resources and capabilities to contribute to a better world and not just build bigger brands?

The results of the 2006 EquiTrend consumer survey of brand equity among US consumers in Ad Age[1] remind me that smart, not money, is what builds brands and behaviors among audiences. Brand equity was measured through quality, familiarity and purchase consideration scores.

Reynolds Wrap, with a $7.5 million annual media budget is the #1 consumer brand among over 1,000 tested with 25,666 respondents. Coke, Pepsi, McDonald's, iPod and Nike - not even in the top ten. Who made it into the top 10? WD-40 (#6 with $25,400 in media spending), Heinz ketchup (#7 with a $413,800 budget), Ziploc bags, Ziploc containers, Clorox bleach, Hershey's candy bars, Kleenex tissues, Windex glass cleaner and Campbell's soups.

A spokesperson explained the #1 ranking by talking about Reynold Wrap's ability to meet consumer's expectations for the product, including its innovations and overall quality. Looking at the Top Ten list I might add that they all serve the person who is confronting the everyday hassles of life by offering simple and predictable solutions.

Some marketers talk about many of these products as 'low involvement' verging on commodity status (who doesn't refer to any glass cleaners as 'Windex' - let alone its iconic status from the movie *My Big Fat Greek Wedding*[2] as a cure for almost anything, 'pass me a Kleenex,' 'he has Ziploc lips about it'). In the social marketing business, we should be so fortunate as to have 'low involvement' behaviors to focus on. After all, health and social change are the most important things in people's lives. Or maybe not. Maybe we make them BIG decisions rather than treat them as the ordinary, everyday behaviors that could be solving some of life's little problems.

Some people want to be like Mike[3] and run a social marketing program with all the bells and whistles. But where is Gatorade on this Top 10 list? I want to be more like Reynolds Wrap - introducing and marketing behaviors that a lot of people think about, reach for and use everyday to make their life, and the lives of those around them, a little better.

Notes

1. https://adage.com/login.php
2. http://www.haro-online.com/movies/my_big_fat_greek_wedding.html
3. Rovell, Darren.(2005).*First in Thirst: How Gatorade Turned the Science of Sweat into a Cultural Phenomenon.* AMACOM.American Management Association. http://www.amanet.org. http://authorviews.com/authors/rovell/rovell-obd.htm

Pardon Me! Advertising

Renting pollution-spewing delivery trucks as moving billboards[1] is the latest gimic in the US city with the worst air pollution (LA).

Mobile Vision Marketing leases trucks and outfits them with global positioning systems to follow the drivers' routes. Clients then choose whether they want to use an empty truck and tailor the route to a targeted audience or, for less money, put ads on the sides of trucks that run pre-scheduled delivery routes.

When one of the owners is asked what people think about the belching smoke from the trucks, he says he doesn't care as long as they see the ad. This is just one of many new examples of interruptive marketing, the term being used by social media advocates to distinguish between the more open, permission-based, and participative philosophy of communication with audiences, not at them. Louise Story looks at advertisers' quest for ubiquity[2] where every blank space is up for bid. Her story contains this nugget about exposure to advertising: the average person living in a city is estimated to be exposed to 5,000 ad messages a day - up from 2,000 30 years ago.

Rohit Bhargava also takes a look at this ubiquity phenomenon, starting with the proposal to allow advertising on the security bins used at airport checkpoints. He goes on to other unexpected places for advertising[3], and suggests the brands to go with them. I suggest the clean air and alternative fuels folks look at those trucks in LA.

The senior VP of marketing for Perry Ellis, quoted in the NYT piece, has it right: *"We're always looking for new mediums and places that have not been used before — it's an effort to get over the clutter,"* Mr. de Echevarria said. *"But,"* he added, *"I guess we end up creating more clutter."*

In the social marketing community we are often trying to emulate our commercial counterparts - even if we don't have the same advertising budgets. Even when we do, this is one arena where it's worth considering the costs and benefits of achieving our own forms of ubiquity and the tone we use to try and achieve it.

Notes

1. http://articles.latimes.com/2007/jan/17/business/fi-mobilead17
2. http://www.nytimes.com/glogin?URI=http://www.nytimes.com/2007/01/15/business/media/15everywhere.html &OQ=_rQ3D2 &OP=Id25b7dcQ2FqsQ60Q5EqQ5CbUQ2F3bbuJqJww9qwiqiQ22q Q5E,Q2FCMQ60Q2FQ2FqQ5BQ60Q5CCtqiQ22Q60!Q603BsYQ60 3Q60oYuQ5Bh
3. http://rohitbhargava.typepad.com/weblog/2007/01/airport_securit. html

All Diets are Created Equal

If you have spent any time in the diet space, whether as a consumer or a professional, you have learned that it is a very confusing place, filled with competing ideologies about what to eat, conflicting scientific evidence about 'bad' foods and 'good' foods, food industry interests undermining pubic policy, and my favorite from personal experience, trying to get four dietitians and nutritionists to agree on essential public health diet recommendations – let alone a roomful of experts. Pile on caveats about cultural factors, sensory experiences, social customs and the dangers of creating more people with eating disorders (to name just a few more), and the reasons for a lack of clear and consistent direction about addressing the obesity epidemic become painfully obvious.

Jennifer Levitz writes in a piece for *The Wall Street Journal*[1] –

You aren't what you eat. You're how much...That's the message from a two-year National Institutes of Health-funded study that assigned 811 overweight people to one of four reduced-calorie diets and found that all trimmed pounds just the same. It didn't matter what foods participants ate, but rather how many calories they consumed. . .The message is that dieting may be "much simpler" than everyone thought, says Catherine Loria, a nutritional epidemiologist at the NIH and co-author of the study. Along with choosing healthful foods, "all you have to do is count your calories." For people who are trying to lose weight, it does not matter if they are counting carbohydrates, protein or fat. All that matters is that they are counting something adds Tara Parker-Pope in *The New York Times*[2].

They are both referring to a study published in *The New England Journal of Medicine*[3]. In the authors' own words:

In this population-based trial, participants were assigned to and taught about diets that emphasized different contents of carbohydrates, fat, and protein and were given reinforcement for 2 years through group and individual sessions. The principal finding is that the diets were equally successful in promoting clinically meaningful weight loss and the maintenance of weight loss over the course of 2 years. Satiety, hunger, satisfaction with the diet, and attendance at group sessions were similar for all diets. The diets improved lipid risk factors and fasting insulin levels in the directions that would be expected on the basis of macronutrient content. The study had a large sample, a high rate of retention, and the sensitivity to detect small changes in weight. The population was diverse with respect to age, income, and geography and included a large percentage of men. The participants were eager to lose weight and to attempt whatever type of diet they were assigned, and they did well in screening interviews and questionnaires that evaluated their motivation. Thus, the findings should be directly applicable to both clinicians' recommendations for weight loss in individual patients and the development of population-wide recommendations by public health officials...Such diets can also be tailored to individual patients on the basis of their personal and cultural preferences and may therefore have the best chance for long-term success.

No doubt the vested interests, from diet book authors to ADM[4] (the largest supplier of high-fructose corn syrup used in most sugared sodas and many other foods), will be trying to rip this study apart. However, from the vantage point of someone who has been involved with a number of public health approaches to weight loss, the words of Aaron Beck[5] come to mind: **Sometimes science is just the validation of common-sense.** [And note that a nutritional epidemiologist is the one quoted as saying 'it is simpler than we thought' – who exactly is WE?]

Now the simple response to this research is to conclude: Let's focus our messages on calories – KISS. That is exactly the 5% solution (See: *Health Communication Campaigns: The 5% Solution*) to avoid. Let's think about this as social marketers (See: *The Change We Need: New Ways of Thinking About Social Issues*):

Audience: Should we focus on children and adolescents (See: Obesity Prevention: What Works) and not tweens (the darlings of the past few years of these efforts)?

Products: How do we make it easier for people to count and track calories? We've had pocket-sized food calorie guides you can look value up in, or web-based systems that do the same. Food diaries to carry around with you or to complete online to detail everything (hopefully) that goes into your mouth. But these clearly have not been enough. What if you could just speak the food items into your phone and then have the calories automatically calculated and entered into a calorie app on your phone, or wirelessly sent to a web site, or appended to your personal health record?

Services: The study had people in counseling sessions over a 2-year period (Group sessions were held once a week, 3 of every 4 weeks during the first 6 months and 2 of every 4 weeks from 6 months to 2 years; individual sessions were held every 8 weeks for the entire 2 years). Anyone who has tried to do that in real life (I wish the authors had described their adherence strategy in the paper) knows the futility of doing this at scale. But, do social and mobile media offer ways around this. And what are the service experiences of participants that lead to long-term commitments to these efforts? Or is it all about the incentives that are offered?

Behaviors: How do we reposition calories against all the other factors that influence people's food choices – convenience, taste, value (amount of food for the dollar), low fat, low carb, organic, pesticide-free? How do we make calorie counting and monitoring easy, fun and popular to do? Remember, we have about 200 opportunities a day to influence food choices. (See: *Designing How We Eat*)

Price: Do we revisit the fat tax idea[6] for calorie dense foods with poor nutritional quality? Tax supersized portion offerings in stores and restaurants? Offer incentives to employer managed food service programs that restrict the availability of high calorie food? Offer reward systems for people who successfully maintain food records or school children whose lunch selections fall within weight/age calorie guidelines? Subsidize health care provider prescribed weight loss counseling?

Place: Limit the proximity of fast food outlets[8] (including convenience stores) to schools? Open school gyms and pools to local residents during after-school hours? Develop mobile apps that identify 'healthy food choice locations' based on your current location? Provide more point-of-choice programs (See: *Diffusion of Calorie Labeling Initiatives*)? Offer more weight loss programs at drug stores? (See: *Drug Store Weight Loss*)

Promotion: Put calorie/serving information on the fronts of food packaging, shelf-labels or tags, and on fast service menu boards (see limits of that approach here[8])? Set up SMS reminder systems of the 'daily menu' designed by the person on their diet website with other eHealth weigh loss tools to be delivered 30 minutes before planned meal times?

Most importantly, we need to understand what are the high leverage behaviors (See: *Can Behavior Change Become Popular?*) that are characteristic of the people who successfully lose weight. As the lead author of the study, Dr. Sacks, said in the NYT article:

The effect of any particular diet group [on weight loss] is minuscule, but the effect of individual behavior is humongous . . . We had some people losing 50 pounds and some people gaining five pounds. That's what we don't have a clue about. I think in the future, researchers should focus less on the actual diet but on finding what is really the biggest governor of success in these individuals.

And maybe some social marketers should be doing so as well. **The bottom line: any low calorie diet leads people to lose weight – we just don't know how they do it.** But as we think about this as a public health issue, and not simply an individual one of a person trying to lose weight, we also need to be cognizant of the other key social determinants that are inherent in our dynamic obesogenic networks (See: *Obesity, HIV and Male Circumcision*) and systems (See: *Behavior Change Amidst Chaos*).

Notes
1. http://online.wsj.com/article/SB123559955210376029.html
2. http://www.nytimes.com/glogin?URI=http://www.nytimes.com/2009/02/26/health/nutrition/26diet.html
3. http://content.nejm.org/cgi/content/full/360/9/859
4. http://en.wikipedia.org/wiki/Archer_Daniels_Midland
5. http://en.wikipedia.org/wiki/Aaron_T._Beck
6. http://calorielab.com/news/2006/01/12/fat-tax-anti-obesity-strategy-debated/
7. http://ajph.aphapublications.org/cgi/content/abstract/99/3/505
8. http://www.ijbnpa.org/content/5/1/63

Demarketing Sugar Consumption in Drinks

Demarketing:[1] Efforts aimed at discouraging (not destroying) the demand for a product which (1) a firm cannot supply in large-enough quantities, or (2) does not want to supply in a certain region where the high costs of distribution or promotion allow only a too little profit margin. Common demarketing strategies include higher prices, scaled-down advertising, and product redesign.

The term came to me as I was reviewing the New York City Health Department campaign, 'Are You Pouring on the Pounds.'[2] The health communication campaign is using outdoor signage and other elements of the communication Ps (PSAs, pamphlets, posters and publicity - oh, and a blog[3] that I am delighted to see has comments turned 'on'!) to raise awareness of sugars in popular beverages and urge New Yorkers to cut back on sugary beverages and quench their thirst with water, seltzer or low-fat milk instead.

I have talked about obesity prevention[4] many times and have outlined how social marketing approaches can be used to address the obesity epidemic[5] beyond the 5% solutions offered by communications programs such as this one.

The NYC project is a start, but if pubic health practice wants to move from simple communication campaigns to more complex and effective marketing ones, they might learn from the tobacco experiences and target the marketing mix, not the people. I am looking forward to reading a new article, "Demarketing tobacco through governmental policies – The 4Ps revisited"[6] in the *Journal of Business Research*. As the authors note in their abstract (unfortunately all the information that is available online)

....governments use anti-smoking advertising to highlight the health risks of smoking and regulatory measures to dissuade consumers from consuming tobacco. In the past, governments tended to take these steps in isolation, now they are more likely to combine these strategies as part of a demarketing mix.

Sounds shockingly (?) familiar to ideas I have talked about with respect to needing new ways to think about and solve wicked problems (See: *The Change We Need*). Perhaps the obesity community could start learning how to develop comprehensive demarketing programs rather than focus on recycling evidence based practices[7] which more often than not stifle innovation and demonstrate how truly behind the times in strategy AND action they really are.

And the Institute of Medicine released a report today with a list of actions that hold the greatest potential to curb obesity rates among children. From the press release[8]:

Many of these steps focus on increasing access to healthy foods and opportunities for active play and exercise. They include providing incentives to lure grocery stores to underserved neighborhoods; eliminating outdoor ads for high-calorie, low-nutrient foods and drinks near schools; requiring calorie and other nutritional information on restaurant menus; implementing local "Safe Routes to School" programs; regulating minimum play space and time in child care programs; rerouting buses or developing other transportation strategies that ensure people can get to grocery stores; and using building codes to ensure facilities have working water fountains.

Gosh that sounds so...marketing (I added the underlines in case you missed them). Better products and services, accessibility and opportunities, incentives, promotion efforts (or reducing the industry's) - that about covers it.

Notes

1. http://www.businessdictionary.com/definition/demarketing.html
2. http://www.nyc.gov/html/doh/html/pr2009/pr057-09.shtml
3. http://pulse.typepad.com/nychealthy/2009/08/cathy-nonas-on-pour-ing-on-the-pounds.html
4. http://socialmarketing.blogs.com/r_craiig_lefebvres_social/obesity_pre-vention/
5. http://socialmarketing.blogs.com/r_craiig_lefebvres_social/2009/02/all-diets-are-created-equal-what-it-means-for-social-marketers.html
6. Shiu, E, Hassan, LM and Walsh, G.(2009). Demarketing tobacco through governmental policies - The 4Ps revisited. *Journal of Business Research*, 62;**2**:269-278.
7. http://www.cdc.gov/Features/HaltingObesity/
8. http://www.nationalacademies.org/onpinews/newsitem.aspx?RecordID=12674

The 4Ps of Demarketing Tobacco Use

Demarketing as a strategy for social marketers is a popular, but unknown or poorly understood part of social marketing practice. Those are my initial conclusions from the feedback and visits to my blog post (See: *Demarketing Sugar Consumption in Drinks*). Popular in that many people are obviously interested in the topic; unknown or misunderstood either because people tell me they have never heard the term before, or thought 'it had something to do with counter-advertising.'

I have talked about how such strategies were employed to frame tobacco control in the NCI ASSIST study[1], and as I noted in the *Demarketing Sugar* post that demarketing tobacco was studied recently by Edward Shiu and his colleagues. Because of the curiosity in demarketing approaches, here is a synopsis from their article to broaden your perspective on this social marketing strategy and how it intersects with many public policy approaches to the topic.

In a social marketing context, they define demarketing as having the objective to decrease demand by discouraging consumption or use of products such as alcohol and cigarettes that pose health risks. They note that while governments use various demarketing strategies and instruments independently to curb smoking (increasing taxes, clean indoor regulations, banning advertising), little research is available on how the 4Ps work in conjunction with each toward reducing tobacco use and how they influence consumer behavior over time.

The authors go on to demonstrate how traditional marketing and demarketing approaches to tobacco can be thought about. Working through the 4Ps, product is framed as product replacement and displacement – most often by offering free or low-cost replacement products (e.g., nicotine replacement therapies) as well as support services (e.g., telephone quit-line and other information services). Increasing taxes and therefore the sales price primarily realigns the price variable. They view place interventions as restricting tobacco consumption opportunities through such instruments as bans on smoking on public transportation and clean-air policies in public places. Promotion interventions are most familiar to readers who lean towards communication approaches to the issue: implementing counter-advertising campaigns, mandatory package warning labels and restrictions on tobacco advertising.

To summarize their overall approach, the authors write:

Conceptualizing the 4Ps from a consumer perspective and linking them to consumer intention via attitudinal mediators is novel and contributes to the literature. Modeling governmental demarketing from a consumer perspective allows one to determine the impact of this government approach not only on consumers' intention to cease consumption, but also on consumer attitudes both toward consuming the product and toward companies that promote and sell these products.

They then go on to develop and test a model of demarketing using data from the International Tobacco Control Four Country Survey[2] - a nationally representative, longitudinal panel survey of adult smokers that was designed to evaluate whether and how a number of key government policy initiatives led to reductions in tobacco consumption. The authors used structural equation modeling to test the hypothesized relationships among policy initiatives aimed at each of the 4Ps, attitudes towards smoking, attitudes towards the tobacco industry, and intentions to quit smoking at two points in time.

The results show that the two attitudinal variables only partially mediated the effects of each of the 4Ps on intention to quit. In each case, the direct effect of each demarketing element on intention is significant over and above the effects of the mediators in the hierarchical regression. The only exceptions to a number of hypotheses about the effects of demarketing strategies on attitudes and intentions were:

1. The demarketing element of product does not affect their attitude toward smoking nor their intention to quit (they suggest that many smokers are already familiar with many of these quit smoking products and services and have already been unsuccessful in using them to quit themselves).

2. Price does negatively affect their attitude toward the tobacco industry (respondents attribute price increases to the industry, not government taxation policies, is their assumption to explain this).

3. The demarketing element place does not affect their attitude toward smoking. Their results demonstrated that governmental demarketing activities during 2002 and 2003 in the U.S. have resulted in significant beneficial changes in smokers' attitude toward smoking and their intention to quit. They conclude:

This study demonstrates the differential effect of the 4Ps of demarketing and the central significance of promotion and price, which are the only demarketing mix elements that influence all three outcome variables, attitude toward the tobacco industry, attitude toward smoking, and intention to quit smoking. At the same time, the empirical evidence from this study shows that the demarketing mix element product, in terms of product replacement and displacement through the promotion of NRT [nicotine replacement therapies] and behavioral support programs, is less effective in terms of changing smokers' attitude toward smoking and intention to quit smoking. Lastly, smoking restrictions at work and in public places do not influence attitude but have a small direct effect on intention to quit.

Two lessons the researchers draw for social marketers are:

1. Social marketers and consumer-policy makers cannot assume individual demarketing measures will be effective in changing the attitudes and behavior of the priority audience. Rather, a comprehensive demarketing mix aimed at decreasing the attractiveness of tobacco and impeding the availability and consumability of cigarettes is needed to result in measurable changes.

2. *Ad hoc* and one-off demarketing measures are unlikely to have the desired effect. The results show an effect over time of the 4Ps of demarketing, suggesting that governments should equip anti-smoking campaigns with sufficient and sustained demarketing resources.

SO when you consider 'upstream social marketing', think demarketing and all 4Ps.

Notes
1. http://socialmarketing.blogs.com/r_craiig_lefebvres_social/2008/10/social-marketing-for-tobacco-control.html
2. http://www.itcproject.org/

The Effects of Media on Health Behaviors

There is widespread appreciation that the media has an influence on health behaviors. In most instances, the perception among public health advocates is that this impact is primarily negative (such as tobacco use, obesity, violence). In a few other cases, the media framing of a health problem is less contentious; what is debated is how to harness the media for improving public health. In the past year, I have heard repeatedly from international HIV prevention experts that *what we need to do is launch the same type of media campaigns to change social norms that the tobacco control community has done*. Unfortunately, this call is then followed by a riff on the need for 'hard-hitting, fear-arousal'-types of efforts. What is unfortunate is that these experts do not appreciate the multiplicity of media efforts that have gone into developing tobacco control media activities – they have not simply been emotional television ads.

The National Cancer Institute has published the monograph The Rise of the Media in Preventing and Reducing Tobacco Use.[1] It should be required reading for anyone using, or considering using, the mass media in any of its forms to address public health issues from obesity to mental illness to climate change. The monograph[2] is a collection of chapters reviewing the empirical evidence on the role of mass media on tobacco use including industry marketing and promotion practices (often the playbook for other industries), tobacco portrayal in news and entertainment media, tobacco control media interventions, and the use of the media by the industry to weaken tobacco control efforts (pay attention to this one too). Here's a sampling of some of the conclusions, pulled from the Executive Summary[3] to start your thinking (my emphasis is added). The key in reading this list, and the monograph, is to make the inference to your own issue and the players and practice that you face. I write this remembering a nutrition professional who after listening to me talk about tobacco advertising and promotion practices and their influence on tobacco use raised her hand and innocently asked: could the food industry do the same thing to encourage excessive consumption, and therefore obesity? Yes they (and others) DO.

- The total weight of evidence - from multiple types of studies, conducted by investigators from different disciplines, and using data from many countries - demonstrates a causal relationship between tobacco advertising and promotion and increased tobacco use.

- Tobacco advertising has been dominated by three themes: providing satis-faction (taste, freshness, mildness, etc.), assuaging anxieties about the dangers of smoking, and creating associations between smoking and desirable outcomes (independence, social success, sexual attraction, thinness, etc.).

- Targeting various population groups - including men, women, youth and young adults, specific racial and ethnic populations, religious groups, the working class, and gay and lesbian populations - has been strategically important to the tobacco industry.

- Substantial evidence exists from the United States and several other countries that tobacco companies typically respond to partial advertising bans in ways that undermine the ban's effectiveness. These responses include shifting promotional expenditures from "banned" media to "permitted" media (which may include emerging technologies and "new" media), changing the types and targets of advertising in permitted media, using tobacco-product brand names for non-tobacco products and services,

- Corporate sponsorship of events and social causes represents a key public relations strategy for major tobacco companies, which spent more than $360 million on these efforts in 2003. Key targets included sporting events, anti-hunger organizations, and arts and minority organizations. These efforts have been used, in certain cases, to influence opinion leaders who benefit from such sponsorship.

- Corporate image campaigns by tobacco companies have highlighted their charitable work in the community and have promoted their youth smoking prevention programs; at times, corporate spending on these campaigns has vastly exceeded the amount actually given to the charities. These campaigns have reduced perceptions among adolescents and adults that tobacco companies are dishonest and culpable for adolescent smoking, and among adults, have increased perceptions of responsible marketing practices and favorable ratings for the individual companies.

- Strong and consistent evidence from longitudinal studies indicates that exposure to cigarette advertising influences nonsmoking adolescents to initiate smoking and to move toward regular smoking.

- The studies of tobacco advertising bans in various countries show that comprehensive bans reduce tobacco consumption. Non-comprehensive restrictions generally induce an increase in expenditures for advertising in "nonbanned" media and for other marketing activities, which offset the effect of the partial ban so that any net change in consumption is minimal or undetectable.

- News coverage that supports tobacco control has been shown to set the agenda for further change at the community, state, and national levels. Despite this, organized media advocacy efforts on behalf of tobacco control issues remain an underutilized area of activity within public health.

- Experimental studies show that images of cigarette smoking in film can influence adolescent and adult viewers' beliefs about social norms for smoking, beliefs about the function and consequences of smoking, and their personal intentions to smoke. Pro-tobacco movie content (e.g., stars smoking, absence of health consequences portrayed) appears to promote pro-smoking beliefs and intentions. The effects observed for experimental studies of smoking in movies on viewers' smoking-related beliefs are of a similar magnitude as those observed in experimental media research on other health topics (e.g., effects of media violence on viewers' aggression).

- The total weight of evidence from cross-sectional, longitudinal, and experimental studies, combined with the high theoretical plausibility from the perspective of social influences, indicates a causal relationship between exposure to movie smoking depictions and youth smoking initiation.

- Numerous studies have shown consistently that advertising carrying strong negative messages about health consequences performs better in affecting target audience appraisals and indicators of message processing (such as recall of the advertisement, thinking more about it, discussing it) compared with other forms of advertising, such as humorous or emotionally neutral advertisements. Some of these negative advertisements also portray deception on the part of the tobacco industry. Advertisements for smoking cessation products and tobacco-industry sponsored smoking prevention advertising have been shown to elicit significantly poorer target audience appraisals than do advertisements based on negative health consequences.

- Population-based studies of anti-tobacco mass media campaigns that were only one component of multi-component tobacco control programs provide considerable evidence for reduced use of tobacco by youth and adults. The anti-tobacco mass media campaign and the other program components together may have reduced smoking more than did any single component alone. The relative contributions of various components to program effectiveness are difficult to determine, but some of the controlled field experiments showed a dose-response relationship between reduced smoking and an increased number of program components.

- Increasing consumer awareness of tobacco industry activities to counteract public-health-sponsored campaigns designed to reduce tobacco use can be an important component of effective media interventions.
- The tobacco industry consistently has used several primary themes to defeat state tobacco tax increase initiatives. These include suggestions that the measures would impose unfair taxes and that tax revenues would not be spent on health care or tobacco control programs as intended. Secondary themes used consistently over an 18-year time span include that the measures would increase "big government" and wasteful spending, discriminate against smokers, and increase crime and smuggling. Other, less frequent themes were that the measures would be a tax cut for the rich, impede economic growth, fail to solve state budget problems, restrict personal choice, and violate antitrust laws.

The point here is with a research base that is probably the most extensive with respect to the role of the media and a health behavior (well, with the exception of the portrayal of aggression on television and violent behaviors[4] which we have known about since the early 1960s), you have to think about media in the broadest possible way – including new media, movies, news coverage, editorial pages and the public policies that govern them (See: *The Policy Making Audience*). It is not just advertisements, entertainment-education or mass media campaigns. I am particularly pleased to see that research in this area is also finding that it is the exposures to multiple channels, (See: *Health Communications Campaigns: The 5% Solution*) rather than the magic bullet[5] that is most likely to lead to behavior change. If researchers would stop asking the wrong question of "which one is it" among a multi-component program and focus instead on how to maximize the impact of media mulitplexity[6], we will move further along the path of developing better interventions across channels that are relevant to our priority audience.

The review also highlights another point I subscribe to: media need to be approached as an agenda-setting tool[7] for policy shifts that encourage healthier behaviors. Changing social norms is an admirable goal, but unless behaviors change and policies are in place to encourage, reinforce and sustain the changes and normative shifts, we are undertaking a Sisyphean task[8]: the norms will always roll back on us after short-lived gains.

[NOTE: The Executive Summary is available in Arabic, Chinese, French, Portuguese, Russian and Spanish.]

Notes
1. http://www.legacyforhealth.org/2667.aspx
2. http://cancercontrol.cancer.gov/tcrb/monographs/19/index.html
3. http://cancercontrol.cancer.gov/tcrb/monographs/19/docs/M19 ExecutiveSummary.pdf
4. http://ceep.crc.uiuc.edu/eecearchive/digests/1997/aidman97.html
5. http://en.wikipedia.org/wiki/Hypodermic_needle_model
6. http://www.allacademic.com/meta/p_mla_apa_research_citation/1/0/6/3/8/p106385_index.html
7. http://en.wikipedia.org/wiki/Agenda-setting_theory
8. http://en.wikipedia.org/wiki/Sisyphus

The Price of Change

The least appreciated part of the marketing mix tool box is price. Social marketers everywhere become easily obsessed with the costs of change - whether it be adopting a new behavior, discontinuing a current one, or using new products or services. Especially in public health the mantra is always *how do we reduce the barriers* to engaging in healthier behaviors. *Rarely do we ask how do we reward people for making healthier choices.* The implicit assumption is that some intrinsic reward mechanism will spontaneously kick in to trigger the cascade of endorphins that will bring them back for more health. Nothing could be farther from the truth as learning theorists (and more recently behavioral economists) will tell you. Here are some recent examples of rewards (aka positive pricing strategies) that could easily have been developed by social marketers - but weren't.

- As part of a larger intervention program offer payments to women who repeatedly test negative for curable sexually transmitted infections[1], such as gonorrhea and syphilis, to reduce unsafe sexual contacts and protect the women not only from the curable STIs but also from contracting or spreading HIV.
- In middle schools in Washington, DC (and other locations in the US), eligible students will be able to earn up to $100 a month[2] for attending class regularly, turning in homework, good behavior and receiving good grades.
- Experiments in offering incentives to providers in order to improve the quality of healthcare[3] are being conducted in Australia, Canada, the United Kingdom and the US.
- Offering smokers $1,000 to quit smoking[4] for a month.

What I encourage you to think about in your programs when it comes to price is not how to reduce them, or even make things easy and free. That's the equivalent of trying to make the punishment less painful for engaging in healthier behaviors. Rather, consider how you might provide incentives for making the healthier choice and reward people when they do. Not only do people learn more quickly this way, but maintenance of the behavior change is likely to be longer lasting as well.

It was stated once that *the challenge of health marketing is in both reducing barriers/ costs of participation and creating incentives that will further engage people in health and behavior change.*[5] One would hope after 20 years that it was getting a little easier and a bit more frequent.

Notes

1. http://blogs.cgdev.org/globalhealth/2008/04/pay-for-prevention-a-1.php#trackbacks
2. http://www.washingtonpost.com/wp-dyn/content/article/2008/08/28/AR2008082803439.html
3. http://www.longwoods.com/product.php?productid=18440&page=6
4. http://www.ncbi.nlm.nih.gov/pubmed/16340515?dopt=Abstract
5. Lefebvre, R.C., Flora, J.A. Social marketing and public health intervention. *Health Education Quarterly*, 1988;**15**:299–315.

Thirty-Five Years of Positioning

The past few weeks have been busy ones for the George Washington University Social Marketing class. We have been experiencing those waves of excitement and foreboding about our client assignments. Trying to not just absorb, but put some meaning to all the information being collected as part of the situation analysis. Grappling with the most difficult question in any social marketing project – who will be our priority audiences?

In the midst of all this (actually at exactly the right time), the reading assignments for the class were the books *Positioning*[1] and *The Brand Gap*[2]. Why the right time? Because now, having settled on priority audiences the big questions of strategy loom. And before creating and executing a marketing plan is the time to consider the branding and positioning platforms for each of our programs. As Marty Neumeier notes in The Brand Gap: *for most of us, brand happens while we're doing something else*. Not this time!

The first articles on Positioning[3] appeared 35 years ago, followed by the book. Reading through it again brought home for me how few marketers of any stripe understand and practice some of its basic tenets. The brands that are discussed as examples of the good, bad, ugly and indifferent stand as great historical context for where marketing was in the 1970's; it also provides as much insight and thoughtfulness for current brand management as it did then. Where would Starbucks[4] and Wal-Mart[5] be if they had read and stuck with the playbook Al Ries and Jack Trout laid out then?

Here are some of the immutable truths I pulled out from a second reading of this classic (personally validated after 20 years of social marketing work):

- The only reality that counts [in positioning and branding] is **what's in people's minds.**
- **Our job as marketers is not communications, it's selection**. You should not try to present all the information about a behavior, product or service to a customer; rather you need to figure out and select what's the most important thing to talk about from the audience POV (positioning).
- Our second job as marketers is to '**cherchez le creneau:**' find the window. The open space – what we called in Consumer-Based Health Communication 'the openings' – *when and where the audience is in the right frame of mind* to be

attentive and receptive to our marketing **and** ready and able to engage in the behavior. Try designing your formative research studies around answering that question!

- *Every ad is a long-term investment in the image of a brand* – substitute the word 'action' for ad, and you get the bigger idea. And **brands aren't 'made' or 'redesigned'** in months or even a few years – logos, slogans and product attributes are.
- *Messages are sounds, not words.* The point being that when print messages are written to be heard - not read, they motivate, inspire and create more lasting impressions (the best demonstrations capture the essence of when radio is referred to as 'the theater of the mind'). Too many times I have seen creative talking reduced to bureaucratic writing by the TUMS practitioners (a term used by a senior manager who admonished her staff before reading some of our ad copy to avoid **Territorial Urinary Marking Syndrome** – translation: keep your pens and pencils in your pockets while you read this!).
- Their discussion of 'repositioning the competition' reminded me how often in social marketing and public health that this is exactly our challenge: **how to reposition people's existing behaviors** into one's they would like to change.

The feedback from students about Positioning has been uniformly exceptional. An easy read that shouldn't be taken lightly. Al Ries is still focused on brands[6]. You can listen to Jack Trout differentiate the marketplace[7].

Notes

1. Ries, A., Trout, J. *Positioning: The Battle for Your Mind.* California: New Riders, 2000.
2. Neumeier, M. *The Brand Gap.* New York: McGraw-Hill, 2005.
3. Searls, D. *The New Character of Positioning Where You Come from Matters More than Where You're Going* (1997). http://www.searls.com/pos.html
4. http://www.slate.com/id/2161504/entry/0/
5. http://www.nytimes.com/2007/03/01/business/worldbusiness/01iht-walmart.4768503.html?_r=2
6. http://www.ries.com/
7. http://www.troutandpartners.com

Perceived Neighborhood Safety

New research[1] finds an independent association between parents' rating of the safety of their neighborhood and the risk of overweight children at the age of seven years. This work, though cross-sectional in nature, lends additional support to the idea that social marketing programs aimed at increasing physical activity among youth should assess, and address if necessary, the potential barriers raised by actual or perceived unsafe neighborhoods.

These data dovetail with two other recent reports from the UCLA Center for Health Policy Research. The first study[2] found that adults in California walk an average of less than one hour per week and one in four do not walk at all during a typical week for transportation or leisure purposes. Researchers found that younger or lower-income adults spend more time walking for transportation while older or more affluent adults spend more time walking for leisure. The amount of walking differed by race and ethnicity, with Latinos walking the most for transportation (72 min/wk) and American Indians/Alaska Natives walking the most for leisure (95 min/wk). Adults in socially cohesive (think 'social capital'), safe neighborhoods with access to parks walk more for leisure than their counterparts. The implications for social marketing interventions aimed at increasing walking, as expressed by the authors were ... *communities that establish safe parks, develop neighborhood crime prevention programs and build social cohesion could increase average leisure walking time by approximately 19 minutes.*

In the second study[3], they report that more teens with access to a safe park get regular physical activity and fewer who have access to a safe park are inactive compared to those who do not have access to a safe park. Access to parks is particularly important for the activity levels of adolescents living in urban areas and for those from low-income families, those living in multi-unit apartment buildings, and those living in neighborhoods perceived as unsafe.

So we can add strategies that increase opportunities to walk (place) and address two specific price variables – social benefits/supports (capital?) and perceived risks of threat/harm – to a comprehensive social marketing program to increase physical activity that only indirectly, yet apparently effectively, may influence the "target" behavior. Who would have thought about neighborhood crime watch programs as an intervention to increase physical activity? And wouldn't you suspect that the presence of such programs is probably influenced by the level of neighborhood cohesion or social capital? Social marketing to enhance social capital - a place that needs a lot more exploration!

Notes

1. Lumeng, J.C., Appugliese, D., Cabral, H.J., Bradley, R.H., Zuckerman, B. Neighborhood safety and overweight status in children. *Archives of Pediatrics and Adolescent Medicine*, 2006;**160**:25-31

2. Brown, R.E., Babey, S.H., Hastert, T.A., Diamant, A.L. Half of California adults walk less than one hour each week. UCLA Health Policy Research Brief, 2005. [http://www.healthpolicy.ucla.edu/pubs/files/AdultWalking_PB_120605.pdf]

3. Babey, S.H., Brown, R.E., Hastert, T.A. Access to safe parks helps increase physical activity among teenagers. UCLA Health Policy Research Brief, 2005. [http://www.healthpolicy.ucla.edu/pubs/files/TeenActivity_PB_120605.pdf]

Social Franchising

One of the shortcomings of social marketing and social change programs is the lack of attention given to their business models. This deficiency is brought into the sunshine when conversations about a program turn to maintaining or sustaining it.[1] These worries are code for 'the grant money is running out and we're not going to get continuation funding from our donor' (whether it is a government agency, philanthropic organization or a corporate or private benefactor). One of the challenges for any social marketing or change program is to develop sustainability.[2] Yet, this often means looking for a new source of funding rather than changing the business model of the program.

Although this problem is by no means restricted to social marketing programs in the developing world, it is here where I see more experimentation with creating sustainable models for interventions and behavior change (or product use). For example, in the past few years there has been a lot of interest in social entrepreneurship,[3] micro-financing[4] and bottom-of-the-pyramid[5] business models as alternatives to the virtual monopoly by the grant-making bodies - though in all fairness, some of these organizations are beginning to stimulate the search for more viable and sustainable[6] approaches to social change.

I came across this post in The Bayesian Heresy[7] that presents another way of thinking about the business of social marketing and social change as practiced by the HealthStore Foundation:[8]

The foundation finds nurses and community health workers who put up a small amount of their own money to buy into a clinic or shop as a franchisee of HSF. The foundation provides up to 88 percent of the capital and gives four weeks of intensive training in marketing and management, as well as some medical training. To recoup capital costs, HSF charges a markup on the essential medicines the clinics sell.

When I think about a franchising model like this, the idea about now being able to build a potentially sustainable program that includes quality control measures[9] and requires the staff to pay close attention to the marketplace, and benefit when they do, is an appealing option. Sure beats the 'we have 2 more years left on this grant, better start writing (a proposal or your resume)' - if you can make it work. But the research needed to figure out better business models and how to transition from one to another in a social change program's life cycle[10] is way behind what the need is.

Says a recent Columbia Business School analysis: "The HealthStore micro-franchise model gives local entrepreneurs the opportunity to own and operate sustainable, profitable businesses while simultaneously curtailing incentives for corruption.... By aligning the incentives of customers, government regulators and owner-operators, HealthStore's franchise model is able to deliver a high quality of care to previously underserved Kenyans while realizing a healthy return on investment."

'A billion mosquito nets served?'

Notes

1. Shediac-Rizkallah, M.C., Bone, L.R. Planning for the sustainability of community-based health programs: conceptual frameworks and future directions for research, practice and policy. *Health Education Research*, 1998; **13**:87-108.
2. O'Loughlin, J., Renaud, L., Richard, L., Gomez, L.S., Paradis, G. Correlates of the sustainability of community-based heart health promotion interventions. *Preventive Medicine*,1998;**27**:702-712..
3. http://en.wikipedia.org/wiki/Social_entrepreneurship
4. http://news.bbc.co.uk/2/hi/business/6047364.stm
5. http://www.12manage.com/methods_prahalad_bottom_of_the_pyramid.html
6. http://www.sustainabilitydictionary.com/
7. http://bayesianheresy.blogspot.com/2007/01/health-franchises-for-africa.html
8. http://www.healthstore.org
9. Rissel, C., Finnegan, J., Bracht, N. Evaluating quality and sustainability: issues and insights from the Minnesota Heart Health Program. *Health Promotion International*, 1995;**10**:199-207.
10. Bowling, C.J. Using the program life cycle can increase your return on time invested. *Journal of Extension*, 2001;**39**(3) [Feature Articles. www.joe.org]

Look for Rodeos

'This ain't my first rodeo'[1] was used by President Bush when he had to work with a Democratic Congress (he had a Democratic State House when Governor of Texas). Today I was reminded of it when looking for venues to get in front of priority audiences. Social marketers often dream of being in the big leagues of professional sports where exposure of a project both in-person and through media coverage can reach into the millions, but the price of admission limits these opportunities to only a few well-funded, or well-connected, programs. However, as you shift your thinking from reach to engagement of social networks and communities, a variety of new options present themselves.

From minor league baseball and hockey to high school teams there are many different ways to interact with social networks and communities when you shift to an audience perspective and think small and targeted. This *Los Angeles Times* story[2] is a case in point.

If Ben Londo's game were football, he'd be as famous as Reggie Bush, the former USC running back who won last year's Heisman Trophy as the country's best college football player.

More famous, actually. Londo, a Cal Poly San Luis Obispo senior, has won his rugged sport's equivalent of the Heisman for two years in a row, and is intent on winning it again this season.

As the article goes on to describe the triumphs of Ben and his college rodeo team, it notes that it costs each team member about $5,000 a school quarter to maintain their horses. And scholarships cover only part of the costs. The visibility of the sport and the needs of the athletes were opportunities US Smokeless Tobacco wasn't going to pass up for its sports marketing portfolio. I wonder how many health promotion programs around the collegiate rodeo circuit have done the same?

The current interest in getting involved in digital social network sites on one hand is quite exciting to witness, but on the other hand there are thousands of social network sites convening every day across the country - sporting, arts and entertainment events in your community - that engage their participants, fans and schools as much (or more) than a site on MySpace. Maybe they don't have the sophistication or Wow! factor of digital media, but these real life social convening points are likely even more powerful than mediated ones to encourage the adoption of the behaviors, products and services you are marketing.

When I was directing a community-based program, our sponsorship of a youth soccer team in the Portuguese community may not have altered a single heart disease risk factor in and of itself, but it paid dividends for us in demonstrating that we were part of their community and developing relationships that led to a series of risk reduction programs (including risk factor screenings at some of the games).

Wherever you are planning or conducting a health promotion program, you might want to ask yourself if this is your first rodeo?[3] And if not, look for one. Speaking of hockey, who wouldn't be conducting some of their flu shot education programs this time of year at ice skating rinks?

Notes
1. http://www.barrypopik.com/index.php/new_york_city/entry/this_aint_my_first_rodeo2/
2. http://articles.latimes.com/2006/nov/21/local/me-rodeo21
3. Crisp, B.R., Swerissen, H. Critical processes for creating health-promoting sporting environments in Australia. *Health Promotion International,* 2003;**18**:145-152.

A City is Full of Stories for Walking

Over dinner in Toronto during a social marketing and social media workshop convened by the Canadian Health Network, the topic turned to mobile thoughts. And I learned about an application of mobile technologies that addresses my regular concern about physical activity advocates recommending 30 minutes of aimless wandering.

[murmur¹] is an archival audio project that collects and curates stories set in specific Toronto locations, told by Torontonians themselves. At each of these locations, a [murmur] sign with a telephone number and location code marks where stories are available. By using a mobile phone, users are able to listen to the story of that place while engaging in the physical experience of being there. Some stories suggest that the listener walk around, following a certain path through a place, while others allow a person to wander with both their feet and their gaze.

Toronto has three [murmur] trails, with others established in Montreal, San Jose (California), Vancouver and the latest addition just launched in Leith, Scotland. As one of our group commented, "It's like being in a museum with the head phones on - except it's our own backyard."
Reminds me of Paths to Health3 with audio. Our next stop is Vancouver.

Notes
1. http://murmurtoronto.ca/
2. http://www.activeliving.org/node/374

Health Communication: The 5% Solution

I was recently asked to present on what are the essential ingredients for a health communication campaign (See: *Health Communications, Social Marketing and Coke*) and what type of impact should be expected from them. For the answer, I turned to Leslie B. Snyder, Ph.D. Professor of Communication Sciences at the University of Connecticut, who has studied the effectiveness of health communication campaigns. In her most recent publication on the subject, she combined the results of several reviews of the literature that together examined over 400 campaigns on a variety of health topics.[1]

Her conclusion: <u>The question isn't whether health communication campaigns are effective – it's what is the average effect size they achieve</u> (how much change do they result in)?

Across all these studies she found that <u>targeted behaviors increase above baseline by an average of about 5 percentage points</u>; a baseline level of a behavior usually is increased, for example, from 60 to 65%. Campaigns for seat belt use (15%), dental care (13%) and adult alcohol reduction (11%) campaigns have had the strongest effects, while youth alcohol and drug campaigns have had the least (1-2%).

Among other risk behaviors that were included in a sufficient number of studies to allow her to arrive at estimates of impact:

- Family planning (6%)
- Youth smoking prevention (6 %)
- Heart disease reduction (including nutrition and physical activity (5%)
- Sexual risk taking (4%)
- Mammography screening (4%)
- Adult smoking prevention (4%)
- Youth alcohol prevention and cessation (4 – 7 %)
- Tobacco prevention (4%)

Preliminary findings on risk behaviors among an even smaller number of studies are that in international breast feeding campaigns the average effect size is $r = .17$ (or 17%), for fruit and vegetable campaigns $r = .08$ and for in-school nutrition programs aimed at 4th-5th graders the $r = .12$.

Obviously, there are several caveats to these conclusions including the reach and frequency of messaging, the audience, the number of channels that were used and differences in measurement and evaluation. However, as a rule-of-thumb, the 5% figure may be a good place to start when you are trying to estimate the impact of a health communications campaign. And another reason to suggest you move beyond IP marketing.

Leslie also found a number of factors that are associated with improved outcomes.

1. Promote adoption of healthier behaviors or substitutions over stopping or preventing unhealthy ones.
2. Habitual behaviors are more difficult to modify than one-off ones (e.g., screening behaviors)
3. Have behavior change as an explicit goal or objective
4. Use formative research in design and planning
5. Focus on homogeneous population groups
6. Communicate directly with your audience and not just through intermediaries
7. Have multiple executions of messages
8. Have a high frequency of exposure to the messages
9. Practice media multiplexity (using multiple channels)
10. Strive for sustained activity to mitigate the observed declines in behavior change after the campaign ends

And at the end of the presentation I added four more rules for developing successful social marketing programs (See: *5 Suggestions to Improve your Social Marketing Program*).

*   Behaviors need to be relevant to audiences – not producers of the message
*   Opportunities and access to engage in new behaviors is necessary
*   Incentives, not barriers, determine behavior change
*   People live in social networks – tap into them

So as you are writing your social marketing plan, some empirically-based places to start.

Note
1. Snyder, L.B. Health communication campaigns and their impact on health. *Journal of Nutrition Education and Behavior*, 2007;*39*:S32-S40.

Bring on Social Media

Speaking of Social Media

Social Media present one of the latest set of opportunities for marketing and communications programs for health promotion and social change. Since I first talked about blending these approaches at the 2007 Social Marketing in Public Heath Conference sponsored by the University of South Florida in Tampa, I have been invited by colleagues at several universities and agencies to reprise elements of it. The presentation has been posted at the conference site along with a number of other highlights from the meetings.

My intention is to present an introduction/overview of Web 2.0, social media and social marketing. Two key goals are to (1) create interest and enthusiasm for trying out new technologies that focus on social networks and not individuals, and (2) encourage adoption of some of these technologies in your professional life.

Some of the key points in the presentation are:

- The often neglected social nature of many health behaviors we focus on in public health interventions.
- How new technologies and software are making social networks more tangible both in terms of interacting with them and measuring results.
- Principles of marketing, such as segmentation, still operate in this new world.
- Audience generated content and engagement is a reality for developing public health programs in this new environment. [Note: this subject is the one that generates the most concern among my audiences.]
- Many people are approaching the new media with the cookie cutters they used before; this needs to change to realize the power of social media to facilitate a multi-directional communication and influence process.

There are also four quotes in the presentation that make up the takeaway:

Web 2.0 sites are not online places to visit so much as services to get something done — usually with other people — Business Week

The Social Web empowers people's ability to engage in self-expression and communicate and share information with whomever they choose — Tech Crunch

Social technologies succeed when they fit into the social lives and practices of those who engage with the technology – danah boyd

It's not about using new technologies; it's about new ways to use technology – Craig Lefebvre

Consider this my first take on the new world of social marketing, social networks and social media. I'll be picking up on several of these themes, and some newer ones, over the next few weeks, including at the National Health Promotion Conference in Atlanta next month. What will you be doing in the new world?

Alternatives to TV Ads and PSAs

Two reports about the commercial and public sectors' exploration of alternatives to 'life as we've known it' for television advertising and public service announcements. From MediaWorks:

Almost 70% of advertisers believe DVRs and VOD will reduce or destroy the effectiveness of traditional 30-second commercials. Instead, they are looking at alternatives such as branded entertainment within TV programs (61%), TV program sponsorships (55%), interactive advertising during TV programs (48%), online video ads (45%) and product placement (44%). Additionally, 80% will spend more of their advertising budgets on Web advertising and 68% are looking into search engine marketing.[1]

The Kaiser Family Foundation held a forum on *New Media and the Future of Public Service Advertising.*[2] A report featuring case studies of projects that have successfully used new media includes: VERB, Fight Mannequinism, Above the Influence, Gain from Gyaan, National Day to Prevent Teenage Pregnancy, Small Steps and Girls Go Tech.

As you would expect, most of these campaigns focused on younger audiences and the use of text messaging, or SMS, as an adjunct to (a) a website and (b) PSAs and paid advertising on television, radio and websites and in various print media. The generic game plan that predominates across these programs is (1) set up a web site with information and/or 'cool stuff' to interact with or download, (2) promote like crazy through traditional media and the web - now it's new!, (3) use cell phones and text messaging as a response channel, (4) push messages and alerts out to participants who opt-in at the web site or through SMS to receive them (you'll recognize this in the proposal as 'permission marketing' - doesn't that feel better?), and (5) measure results by eyeballs and click throughs.

Not exactly 'new' in many cases, though I did see some glimmers of audience generated content (See Blog Post: Generation C) in a few programs and viral messages for SMS. More like old wine (creative for the old media) poured into some 'new' bottles.

There are some understandable concerns about engaging with new media - especially by government agencies - that have [a lot] to do with losing control of messages and their distribution. The emergence of new media, and particularly social media, enables users to connect with people and create, repurpose and mashup content to establish and strengthen social networks. It is the antithesis of the 'top down' or inoculation model of communications practiced by the advertising community and so many of its imitators in the public and nonprofit sectors. Here's a place to start thinking about how to use social media that is also 'technology free' - old fashioned interpersonal communications is still the driver of behavior change.[3] *It's not about using new technologies, it's about new ways to use technology.*

The promise of social media lies in its ability to empower audiences rather than continuing to transform them into passive vessels into which we are trying to 'pour' our messages. The saying that 'public health has messages while people have lives' is one to take to heart as you consider using the new media in your programs. Employ the technologies as your audience are using them in their daily lives, not as an extension of radio and television formats. Perhaps someone is working on the 2006 version of the "1984" Apple commercial to depict the shift from old to new media? Pick up you hammer.

Notes
1. Klaassen, A. Marketers lose confidence in TV advertising. *Advertising Age*, March 22, 2006.
2. http://www.kff.org/entmedia/upload/7469.pdf
3. http://decker.typepad.com/welcome/2006/03/5_tips_to_marke.html

Social Media in a Crisis

A rhetorical question I posed at the end of our Blogging for Public Health session at CDC in April 2007 that was intended to generate a sense of urgency to become involved in the social media space took on some chilling realities with the events at Virginia Tech.[1] Susan Promisio captured it like this:[2]

'What if the post-9/11 anthrax scare happened now instead of then?' If the CDC isn't out in front in the blogosphere, owning that issue and guiding the public in how to interpret the threat and respond appropriately, other bloggers who might be less expert, but quicker to capitalize on the information vacuum, will command the blogging stage.

Marianne Richmond, another of our panelists, weighs in about the VT tragedy from that same perspective.[3]

Yesterday's incomprehensible tragic events at Virginia Tech also highlight the way the information is disseminated during a crisis and the need for "official" sources to use social media tools as part of their crisis management plan. I think one of the thoughts that became crystallized for me during the CDC panel and the Forrester Marketing Forum is that if social media was viewed in light of this is a tool, what can I use it for to enhance my communications...

And that mobile technologies were not part of the official response to notify students of danger is another signal that taking a head-in-the-sand approach to emergency risk communications using old media (email !?) endangers lives for control of the message. I don't think that's a reasonable trade-off. And ignorance is no longer an excuse.

Notes
1. http://en.wikipedia.org/wiki/Virginia_Tech_massacre
2. http://rwjfblogs.typepad.com/pioneer/2007/04/pioneering_idea.html
3. http://www.blogher.com/node/18387

Bridging the New Media Culture Chasm:
Can Elephants Dance?

The recent attempt by Johnson & Johnson 'to engender sympathy and appreciation for all that parents do for their kids…through an attempt at humor' in an online ad for the OTC pain-killer Motrin, was met by a predictable blowback from women across the blogosphere, on YouTube and on Twitter who found it an insensitive portrayal of women's pain (in the ad, the pains are from carrying their baby in slings). The ad was quickly pulled, apologies were made and a threatened boycott of the product is seemingly avoided.

For people who are engaged with new media, the story reinforces for them how potent the voice of the people formerly known as the audience can be and how quickly people can be mobilized with social media. For pharmaceutical companies, nonprofit organizations and government agencies still contemplating a move into new media, the story reinforces their worse fears: loss of control over the message, negative feedback and criticism, threats to integrity and self-generated brands (as opposed to ones that are co-created with users). In short, more reinforcement for reasons to not join the dance.

As social marketers, we can also ask: who tested the ads to begin with? But more importantly, did they test the ads with the right people? Testing of this message, or any others intended to be viewed online, needs to be done with the people who will see the message – not 'mothers,' but mothers who are online and likely to come across it. And why the 'mommy bloggers' weren't part of the J&J strategy to start with was…well…so…atavistic. Maybe like testing television ads in the 1950s with radio audiences. Using monolithic racial and ethnic models in ads in the 1970s. And do not overlook the fact that the J&J ad was suppose to be humorous. Yes, trying to make things appear fun and use humor can be as tricky as when to use fear appeals in campaigns.

How do we help organizations move into the new media space when they can quickly latch onto these types of stories as another reason 'why not?' Coincidentally, or not, *The Wall Street Journal* today tells the story of a new type of collaboration between P&G (the iconoclastic consumer marketing organization) and Google, one that involves an employee exchange program. About 2 dozen employees are sitting in on the other's training and strategy meetings, learning the culture in ways that will (hopefully for Google) lead P&G to invest more ad dollars in online media where they are well behind the curve among major brands spending an estimated 2% of their marketing budget for online, and (hopefully for P&G) enhances their marketing to younger consumers and helps them avoid the pitfalls and be as smart about online marketing as they are about the rest of it.

As the two companies started working together, the gulf between them quickly became apparent. In April, when actress Salma Hayek unveiled an ambitious promotion for P&G's Pampers brand, the Google team was stunned to learn that Pampers hadn't invited any "motherhood" bloggers — women who run popular Web sites about child-rearing — to attend the press conference.

"Where are the bloggers?" asked a Google staffer in disbelief, according to one person present.

Later in the story we learn that P&G eventually did invite a group of bloggers to their baby division in Cincinnati for a tour and meetings with executives. The results, claim the bloggers, was between 100,000 – 6,000,000 visitors to their Web sites.

In a video documenting these meetings, Pampers spokesman Bryan McCleary says, *This is a very different type of communication than what Procter & Gamble is used to . . . [The bloggers] don't like advertising. What they do like are exciting stories ... and those things actually can become word-of-mouth advertising, if done in the right way.*

Among some other stories: the discovery that searches with the word 'coupons' are up 50% in the past year; trying a spoof video contest of P&Gs Talking Stain ad (with some controls in place, but still a radical experiment in consumer-generated content); and learning about their common philosophy for in-store and online ads. And then there where the eye-openers for Google staff:

P&G employees gasped in surprise during a Tide brand meeting when a Google job-swapper apparently didn't realize that Tide's signature orange-colored packaging is a key part of the brand's image (do not mess with the colors of a $2.5 billion brand).

SO what is the takeaway here? Well, organizations have a right to, and certainly have anecdotal evidence to support, being cautious about excursions into the new media space. Yet, with changing demographics and media usage patterns, you also have a responsibility to explore, experiment and engage with new media. And maybe the right way to do this is not the old way of hiring agencies, having meetings, exchanging documents, and having more meetings. Maybe the P&G/Google model is correct: work side-by-side in each other's natural habitat and learn how the cultures need to adapt to the new technology — not simply how to adapt the tools. Then you can produce work that meets and even exceeds the expectations of people. As I have said before, <u>it is not about using new technology, it is about new ways to use technology</u>. The old way of talking at people may be comfortable, but check in with J&J and others to see if it still works.

And for the managers in some of these organizations who may need some inspiration - Who says elephants can't dance?

Notes
1. http://blogs.wsj.com/health/2008/11/17/jj-gets-caught-in-a-sling-over-internet-motrin-ad/
2. http://online.wsj.com/article/SB122705787917439625.html

Open Source Epidemiology

If you work in a public health agency, the next time you are trying to make a case for using social media, or even more radical, developing open source wikis for your agency (See: *The Secret Uses of Wikis and Blogs*) or social marketing program, be sure you have a copy of this article from the *Los Angeles Times*[1] in hand. Many administrators in these agencies are physicians, and often epidemiologists, by training. While they might appreciate the value of a good sound bite, they often have a difficult time relating to social marketing, and the notion of 'losing control' over communications with social media is frightening (they won't say that, but it is!).

The article describes ProMED[2], a free, open source and access website that is the Wikipedia of disease surveillance.

In 2003, ProMED was first to report the disease that turned out to be severe acute respiratory syndrome, or SARS. Though China initially tried to squelch news of the mysterious outbreak, Madoff says, ProMED tracked the spread of the disease. When ProMED fans at a Toronto hospital began seeing symptoms similar to what they were reading on-line, they isolated suspect patients and took other steps now credited with having limited its spread.

The service also won fans in October 2001 during the anthrax letter attacks that killed five, infected 17 and put more than 20,000 frightened Americans on antibiotics. D.A. Henderson, the scientist who led the successful campaign to eradicate smallpox and who was then a key advisor to the secretary of Health and Human Services, said CNN and ProMED had been the government's most reliable sources of information.

Quite a track record and high praise for an open source approach to knowledge development and management, and maybe something that will resonate with those managers and colleagues who still think the laboratory, randomized clinical trials and tortured clearance procedures are the path to truth and wisdom. You might also be able to open them up to the idea that social media and open source projects lead to a heightened ability to sense and respond to changes in the real world rather than having less control.

There are other internet systems for disease outbreaks available, such as Global Public Health Intelligence Network,[3] which does real-time monitoring of media in seven languages. However, it only monitors news media outlets and lacks a complete open source component (where anyone can contribute to it at any time). You can also intrigue your epidemiologist colleagues with the blue sky discussion of INSTEDD, the International System for Total Early Disease Detection, at LunchoverIP[4] and the 'what ifs?' of adding human inputs to these more automated systems. Then maybe they'd start to get it.

Now, about that marketing idea we have...

Notes

1. Miller, J. Website for the germ-obsessed. *Los Angeles Times*, 13 January 2007 [http://www.latimes.com/news/opinion/la-oe-judymiller-13jan13,0,6444591.story?track=tothtml]
2. http://www.promedmail.org/pls/otn/f?p=2400:1000:
3. http://www.phac-aspc.gc.ca/media/nr-rp/2004/2004_gphin-rmispbk-eng.php
4. Giussani, B. Larry Brilliant's InSTEDD: Can the Internet help stop pandemics? http://giussani.typepad.com/loip/2006/03/can_the_interne.html

Molecular Marketing

Imagine the ability to create your own multi-media campaigns from professionally developed source materials that you then customize to your local situation, weather conditions and even the live action on a television show before the commercial break. This evolution to virtual advertising and marketing,[1] think enabling user-generated productions by campaign and program managers, is now going prime time.

Several companies are offering automated ad creation over the Internet, and in some cases, ad placement services that all advertisers can use to more tightly focus their marketing. Advertisers use the new sites to select scenes from commercial films and customize campaigns with a few clicks of the mouse and little human interaction, often for a low flat fee.

Imagine that your issue is the focus of a national social marketing campaign by a government or nonprofit agency. Rather than being handed prerecorded PSAs, pdf files and the like, instead you are given access to the content itself with the freedom to customize it as you like, combine it with your own content, and distribute it in ways that fit the openings of your local priority audiences. Now that sure beats the passive and reactive posture many of us have found ourselves in when national campaigns suddenly 'show up' in our markets with no obvious hooks to our agencies or context. But, will these national organizations and their advertising and PR agencies be willing to give up that much control? Not until we ask.

"We're moving into a world of molecular marketing," said Bant Breen, director of strategic development and innovation for the Interpublic Group..."This is an opportunity for creatives to do what they've always wanted to do, which is to speak in a more powerful way to each and every consumer."

Take a tour of what could be in your future. This site is for car dealerships right now;[2] here's another that lets central command provide some tailoring to local markets or different audience.[3] Let your imagination soar.

It's another evolution in entrusting the power of marketing with the people who are closest to the audience.

Notes

1. Story, L. Ads made by you, in a click. *New York Times*, 8 February 2007. http://www.nytimes.com/2007/02/08/business/media/08adco.html?_r=4&pagewanted=1&adxnnl=0&ref=technology&adxnnlx=1170964229-4sstyfJ4jBy2utNiCp0drQ
2. https://www.pick-n-click.com/
3. https://www.visibleworld.com/creative/solution.php

Social Media, Mind Melding and Health

The connection between social support networks and a variety of health and medical conditions is well documented[1] (see also *Social Support and Physical Health*[2]). The nature of health care provide-patient communications and its relation to health outcomes has also received much attention in the health care literature.[3] How these social networks and interpersonal relationships actually influence health and medical outcomes is less well understood. Daniel Goleman offers an intriguing look at social neuroscience in the *New York Times*.[4]

The most significant finding was the discovery of "mirror neurons," a widely dispersed class of brain cells that operate like neural WiFi. Mirror neurons track the emotional flow, movement and even intentions of the person we are with, and replicate this sensed state in our own brain by stirring in our brain the same areas active in the other person.

Mirror neurons offer a neural mechanism that explains emotional contagion, the tendency of one person to catch the feelings of another, particularly if strongly expressed. This brain-to-brain link may also account for feelings of rapport, which research finds depend in part on extremely rapid synchronization of people's posture, vocal pacing and movements as they interact. In short, these brain cells seem to allow the interpersonal orchestration of shifts in physiology...

...the emotional status of our main relationships has a significant impact on our overall pattern of cardiovascular and neuroendocrine activity.

As we look at the role social media can play in public health and health care, it is important to remember that it is not just a set of tactics we are exploring, but a way of thinking about health behaviors that focuses on understanding, enabling and expanding social networks. After all, getting screened for asymptomatic illnesses and medical conditions (high blood pressure, breast or cervical cancer), modifying one's lifestyle to lose weight or be more physically active, stop engaging in addictive behaviors such as cigarette smoking and substance abuse, complying with regimens to treat and manage conditions from HIV to diabetes, and adopting behaviors to prevent unintentional injuries (seat belt use, fall prevention in the elderly) all involve social networks - spouses, other family members, relatives, friends, co-workers, other patients, etc...

That there may be biological mechanisms to explain how social networks influence our health strengthens the argument to understand the world of social media. The more we learn about social networks and how to engage them for health improvement and health promotion, the more opportunities we can offer to people to enable them to live productive and satisfying lives.

The next time you catch yourself mirroring someone, are they healthy vibes?

Notes
1. CDC. Social support and health-related quality of life among older adults — Missouri, 2000. *Morbidity and Mortality Weekly*, 2000; 54; 433-437. [http://www.cdc.gov/mmwr/preview/mmwrhtml/mm5417a4.htm]
2. Uchino, B.N. (2004). *Social Support and Physical Health Understanding the Health Consequences of Relationships*. New Haven: Yale University Press, 2004.
3. Duggan, A. Understanding interpersonal communication processes across health contexts: Advances in the last decade and challenges for the next decade. *Journal of Health Communication*, 2006;11:93-108.
4. Goleman, D. Friends for life: An emerging biology of emotional healing. *New York Times*, 10 October 2006. [http://www.nytimes.com/2006/10/10/health/psychology/10essa.html?ex=1318132800&en=f5903ea6882cfa9d&ei=5089&partner=rssyahoo&emc=rss]

Developing Social Media Strategies

The strategic use of social media is about changing your perspective, not using new communication tools. The talks I give about social media and social marketing these days focus almost exclusively on the shift we need to make in how we think about interacting with people formerly known as the audience and much less on the tactics, or how to use specific social and mobile media tools. Fortunately, in the past four years, many social marketers and change agents have emerged to fill in those gaps. But the pace of adoption of social media in public health and social marketing programs is outpacing the understanding that social media is not simply a new set of communication tools to substitute for, or complement, posters, pamphlets, PSAs and publicity events (See: *Health Communications, Social Marketing and Coke*).

A number of points about strategy and social media came together for me over the past few days as I have been consulting on five different social media projects at various stages of development. The contours of the issues each project faces are specific to the environment they are percolating in, but the repetitive themes that kept coming to the foreground – and my response to them, equally repetitive - brought me to writing a few of them down to share here.

The issues revolve around the self-defining question of <u>what should be the role of a sponsoring organization when launching social media efforts</u>?

The default positions most people gravitate towards come from the old model of communications – develop 'innovative' or 'pilot" projects that use various social media tools (usually Facebook, Twitter and widgets, maybe a blog – rarely a mobile strategy or MySpace and never a wiki, building relationships with bloggers or working with existing local social network sites). A few groups recognize the value of co-creation of content, but have little idea of where to start and have the expected jitters about how all that will work out IF they were to try it. Somehow many people become amnesic that we have always had essay, photo, poetry and other types of contests to elicit content from ordinary people. Somehow, it has become sooo – sinister, subversive, sexy?

A slightly more enlightened position to assuming the familiar role of content creator is to become the expert consultants or coaches for others – provide training and technical assistance to the newbies in the organization, state, or whatever. What will they teach? Mostly how to use the new media in old ways.

<u>What I believe are the more powerful positions to take</u>, and here I mean by powerful the strategies that exploit the features of the social media, and not simply put old wine into new bottles, <u>are to become collaborators, conveners, facilitators, brokers and weavers</u>. By collaborators, I mean working inside what others have created – existing blogs, social network sites; creating platforms for group participation from the beginning – not just as a glorified dissemination website. By conveners I think about using social media in new ways to bring people of common purpose together to get things done – not simply substitute computer-mediated (not even in Second Life) meetings for in-person ones (aka the burgeoning scheduling of 'webinars') to 'talk.' One of the major barriers to becoming a convener is that few people and organizations understand the effort that must go into changing the behaviors of their collaborators.[1] Becoming a dynamic resource center – not a place where people go to check out job posts, download toolkits and case studies, but where people can, among other things, exchange advice and information, solicit creative work, comment on works in progress, allow agencies to see who outside their usual networks might have the ways and means to reach priority groups.

For example, why do so few health programs reach poor, underserved and rural populations through agricultural extension services? Why do federal health agencies work so closely with state health departments for pandemic flu preparedness when they clearly do not achieve the presence that is necessary for an informed public and prepared and responsive smaller public health agencies (is there some presumption of trickle-down communication)?[2] And finally, agencies and organizations need to think about themselves as network weavers[3] – pulling together what are usually (when you look for them) a number of diverse and isolated groups working on the same problem but do not have the connectors, or bridges, to bring them into contact with one another. When I suggest creating a collaborative platform for the program, the default response is to move all the usual suspects onto it – and not see it as the way to engage the local groups, advocates and affected groups in the effort. Their response is - how will we manage all of them?! Maybe a first step is to believe in the power of groups and social networks to self-organize. But that's another story for another post.

Using social media means embracing the idea that the world is composed of social networks, not individuals (See: *Maybe IT IS ALL about Social Networks*). In my talks I distinguish between the old world of sources, channels, messages and receivers (a convenient fiction reinforced by the dominance of broadcast media for several decades) and the new world of distributed social media where anyone can be a producer and distributor of information. This new world focuses us on the engagement of people, not trying to creatively break through clutter; the idea that people are continuously interacting with each other and yes, will talk back to you (the secret is they always were, you just could not hear them); and the need for multiplexity – that in the new world of masses of media, and the personalization of one's media environment, it is ubiquity that is important – not being on Facebook or Twitter. And yes, I do see people creating tactic-driven strategies. It goes like this: we want to use Twitter – or some other social media tool - because it's cool, or someone really wants us to, or everyone else is doing it. So how can we rationalize it by creating a strategy that makes sense for us to use it? Forget what the original objectives of the campaign were – we can change those too. You get the circularity of the argument.

Understanding that it is a social world means shifting our thinking from individuals to the connections between them. As I put it today, <u>focus on using social media to take advantage of the connections people have with each other, not to reach people in new ways</u>. What we find when we do this is the challenge of 'making something go viral' – a core wish of all social media toolmakers – becomes more clear. <u>The challenge has to be framed: how do we design experiences people want to share, rather than simply how do we design something that is entertaining and changes their behavior</u> (whoops, that old mentality slipping in again). That is how behavior and culture can be shaped, changed, shifted. Through people exchanging with each other. And once you get to that place – that we all live in a marketplace of ideas, behaviors, products and services (See Blog Post: *The Change We Need: New Ways of Thinking About Social Issues*). That people we wish to serve are not a horde of individuals only calculating costs and benefits for behaving (performing?) in self-interested ways. But people forming and participating in any number of social networks through shared social objects[4], beliefs, customs, norms that in turn influence their and our behaviors.

Some of those people we used to call audiences, and others we call our co-workers and partners. Others are people working in what use to be thought of as disparate fields, agencies and lands. New technologies have made it clearer than the theorists ever could that we are all connected in many different ways. Social media gives us the tools to discover and transform these relationships, not just pay rhetorical homage to intersectoral collaboration, busting out of silos, reaching across departments and offices, nurturing and sharing collective wisdom and experience (wherever it may be), engaging the public and building social capital, and leveraging scarce resources. But first it means <u>as social marketers that we need to think about social media as a means for pursuing social strategies for making the world a better place for all the people that live in it. And then as a way to transform how we go about doing our work.</u>

Notes

1. Preece, J. Shneiderman, B., The reader-to-leader framework: Motivating technology-mediated social participation. *AIS Transactions on Human-Computer Interaction*, 2009;1:13-32. [http://aisel.aisnet.org/thci/vol1/iss1/5/]
2. Ringel, J.S., Trentacost, E., Lurie, N. How well did health departments communicate about risk at the start of the swine flu epidemic. *Health Affairs*, 2009;28:w743-w750. [http://content.healthaffairs.org/cgi/content/abstract/hlthaff.28.4.w743]
3. http://networkweaver.blogspot.com/
4. http://gapingvoid.com/2007/10/24/more-thoughts-on-social-objects/

Avoiding 8 Deadly Sins of Social Media Programs

Chris Aarons and Geoff Nelson look at failed social media campaigns and make this list of suggestions to avoid the common problems and expectations people have when embarking on social media efforts.[1]

1. *Good strategy results in viral, but viral is not a strategy.*
2. *What someone says about you is more important than what you say about yourself.*
3. *People are already motivated to do many different things. By identifying where their motivation intersects with yours, you can avoid creating a contrived campaign. However, if you are ready and able to compensate people for their effort, the likelihood of participation goes up exponentially.*
4. *Money isn't the best social currency; relationships and knowledge are.*
5. *PR is great for news and launches, but social media creates the ongoing and sustained interest between news and launches.*
6. *Buying advertising space on social media sites doesn't return a quarter of the value you could be getting. Further, the costs of the campaign drive up the ROI bar you need to justify it.*
7. *Social media sites, people, and applications have vastly differing capabilities. Random, unplanned usage of these tactics will deliver poor results.*
8. *Social media is a strategic amplifier for your campaign, not the entire campaign.*

Note
1. http://www.imediaconnection.com/content/23906.asp

Fallacies of Buzz Builders

What is often passed off as 'the new way' of building word-of-mouth or buzz, social computing[1] or social marketing[2] is mostly *the old wine of a broadcasting model of communication being repackaged in the new bottles of social networks*. The strategy remains the same, only the tactics differ. Now instead of crafting messages to be delivered through third-party, passive media pipelines, many marketers focus on crafting messages to be delivered through authentic, proactive ones (participants, users, consumers). I refer to this as 'the old world' way of continuing to view communication as a linear process of Source-Message-Channel-Receiver that still dominates most marketing communications in the 'new' social media world.

BrandWeek[3] has an interview with sociologist Duncan Watts who challenges the precepts of connectors and mavens popularized by Gladwell in The Tipping Point[4] as well as the notion that finding and priming influencers is the ticket to successful buzz making. In fact, the opposite may be true.

BW: How would you advise a marketer to act if they want to start a buzz?

DW: First, they should focus less on who people influence and more on how people are influenced. It sounds like just the other side of the same coin, but the difference is important—identifying easily influenced people, and how they are influenced raises different questions, and requires different research design than looking for influentials. Second, they should also think more about networks, and network structure, rather than treating everyone as behaving independently. And third, they should move away from the idea that buzz can be engineered to achieve some prespecified outcome, and get better at measuring and reacting to buzz that arises naturally.

It is a new world of thinking about how to do communications, not just changing [our] communication behaviors. Yet, as I like to point out in my presentation, it is not how communication works that has changed in the past few years, new media have just made it more obvious. The power is, and has always been, in the networks.

Notes

1. Li, C. Forrester's social computing report. *Groundswell Blog*, 17 February 2006   [http://forrester.typepad.com/groundswell/2006/02/forrsters_socia.html]
2. Bernoff, J. Social marketing with tweens. *Groundswell Blog*, 24 January 2007 [http://forrester.typepad.com/groundswell/2007/01/social_marketin.html]
3. http://www.brandweek.com/bw/news/packaged/article_display.jsp?vnu_content_id=1003553675
4. http://www.gladwell.com/tippingpoint/index.html

The Secret Uses of Wikis and Blogs

Addressing the barriers and answering the protests about using social media and collaborative tools cannot be any more difficult than in the spy business. In the Sunday New York Times Magazine, Clive Thompson reports on how the US intelligence community has been incorporating blogs and wikis into the way they do business.[1]

Among the points made in the article that you can apply to your situation, whether it is in a corporate, public or nonprofit setting working with any health or social issue are:

The need to focus on the challenges posed by your organizational culture even more than the technologies to make them work for you. *He was also up against something deeper in the DNA of the intelligence services. "We've had this 'need to know' culture for years," Meyerrose said. "Well, we need to move to a 'need to share' philosophy."*

Designing the innovations of using wikis and blogs to be quickly and broadly adopted by a critical mass of workers (early adopters and early majority) and not just a few fashion-setters or geeks. *For the intelligence agencies to benefit from "social software," he said, they need to persuade thousands of employees to begin blogging and creating wikis all at once. And that requires a cultural sea change: persuading analysts, who for years have survived by holding their cards tightly to their chests, to begin openly showing their hands online.*

Acknowledging and working with the 'traditionalists' or 'laggards' in your organization who, for better of worse, are often in critical positions to influence whether innovations are introduced in the first place. *The resistance comes from the "iron majors" — career officers who occupy the enormous middle bureaucracy of the spy agencies. They might find the idea of an empowered grass roots to be foolhardy; they might also worry that it threatens their turf.*

As you think about introducing social media into your organization, or are just beginning to do so, the examples from the intelligence community may help persuade some of your colleagues of their untapped potential. But also remember that it is a diffusion of innovations process in an organizational setting. Follow what we know about diffusion theory and you are likely to be much more successful and avoid a number of headaches along the way.

And for some additional resources about wikis, See Working with Wikis in this book for some of the interpersonal and management issues you need to plan for and the wikimatrix site[2] that can help you choose from among the many wiki platforms that are currently available.

Notes
1. http://www.nytimes.com/glogin?URI=http://www.nytimes.com/2006/12/03/magazine/03intelligence.html
2. http://www.wikimatrix.org/

Working with Wikis

Elizabeth Albrycht posts on 'Thinking About Wikis'[1] at the Society for New Communications Research blog as a prelude for a research study on the use of wikis among knowledge workers in creative roles. Over the past few weeks several of us have been putting together a social marketing wiki.[2] I was surprised to find that she considers us among the early adopters of this technology for community collaboration and knowledge management. Here are some of her thoughts from a preliminary review of research on collaboration.

- *How do you encourage individuals to contribute their knowledge when it is a primary factor in the way they are evaluated and rewarded? The latter leads to knowledge hoarding to increase value vs. knowledge sharing, which is what collaborative systems are designed, at heart, to do.*
- *How do you deal with group dynamics in order to keep participants productive?*
- *How can the collaborative technology be designed to be a part of an employee's work process vs. an add-on system?*
- *How can you best support the learning curve demanded by the technology?*

Her group has also distilled seven factors that seem to be critical for success in designing and implementing a wiki.

1. Support of Reputation Development
2. Clear Procedures of Management and Discipline
3. Defined and Followed User Responsibilities
4. Content: Knowledge Creation and Decision Making
5. Group Attributes
6. Effective Wiki Design
7. Training/Convincing People

I invite you to read her post - and be sure to check some of the online references at the end of it. Then join our social marketing wiki experiment in using social media to enhance all our abilities to do bigger and better social change programs.

Notes
1. http://www.newcommblogzine.com/?p=408
2. http://socialmarketing.wetpaint.com/

Going Mobile for a Change

When you look at your cell phone, what do you see? More important, what do you think about?

Text messaging (or SMS), especially among teens and young adults, is part of the bigger picture. Using the phone as a camera is becoming popular as well (I've seen references that 44% of people use their mobile as their primary camera). And with virtually all mobiles being SMS-capable and web-enabled by 2009 (it's about 94% and 41% now), the question becomes how these technologies might contribute to positive social and health change.

Since ways of interacting with and among social networks for public health and social change has re-ignited my imagination, I have been looking at how other people have been using mobile phones for things other than consumer marketing and entertainment. One belief I do have is that mobile phones are one of the most, if not most, important everyday gadgets that almost everyone has access to [and in most of the world, cell phone use is leapfrogging[1] hard lines]. NOT exploring their use is a form of social marketing and health communications malpractice.

Here are a few places I've discovered that have stimulated my thinking in this area.

A Post at SmartMobs[2] notes a UK study documenting the many other uses people find for their mobile phones including citizen journalism and increasing personal safety at night. *Mobumentaries - people using their phones to create mini-movies documenting their lives.*

Thoughts about mobile technologies[3] and social change movements that were also covered here (See: *Social Networking and Social Activism*): *The combination of MySpace and cell phones, along with some old fashioned fliers, were credited with organizing the large student protests against the proposed immigration bill in March. Just imagine if while at the marches, students posted photos, videos, and text messages to a social networking website or to the website of a group organizing against the bill, and they also sent these messages to all their online friends.*

A literature review of mobile technologies and learning at Futurelab:[4] *Mobile technologies are a familiar part of the lives of most teachers and students in the UK today. We take it for granted that we can talk to other people at any time, from wherever we may be; we are beginning to see it as normal that we can access information, take photographs, record our thoughts with one device, and that we can share these with our friends, colleagues or the wider world. Newer developments in mobile phone technology are also beginning to offer the potential for rich multimedia experiences and for location-specific resources.*

The University of Sydney, Australia hosted an international conference on social and cultural aspects of mobile phones, convergent media, and wireless technologies 2-4 July 2007.[5] Having become an important technology for voice and text communication in the daily lives of billions of people, mobiles are now recognised as central not only for communications but also for contemporary transformations in cultural and social practices, and in new developments in computing, media, telecommunications, Internet, and entertainment.

From a more commercial perspective, here's an introduction to, and overview of, the Mobile Marketing[6] movement; and keep up with events in the field at the Mobile Marketing Association[7] site. Also see these links to examples[8] of three commercial mobile marketing campaigns, including one for McDonald's.

Nedra Weinreich has also been talking about cell phones and social marketing at Spare Change.[9] One of the pioneers in using the technology at the local level has been the San Francisco Department of Public Health and their SexInfo text messaging system for sexual health.[10] The use of mobile technologies for obesity management has also received a lot of empirical attention.

And some blogs that focus on mobile applications for education, engagement and behavior change you may want to check in with periodically are Mobile Learning,[11] Mobile Active,[12] and Captology Notebook[13] where they are compiling examples of mobile persuasion technologies in their Boomer Mobile Health Project. The Stanford University Persuasive Technology Lab also hosted a conference on mobile persuasion.[14]

And for a glimpse of the future, Cingular and Sprint wireless customers can watch the Emmy's live via GoTV.[15] {Sigh} I won't be upgrading my mobile until the end of the year (Verizon incentive policy for replacements), so in the meantime I'm experimenting with Google's SMS service and Yahoo! Mobile alerts. . . and looking for a few peers who aren't too old to try new tricks and experiment with some new ideas. One of my favorites is mobile enabled walksheds.

m(mobile)-Change. The next time you look at your phone.

Notes
1. Gupta. V. Envisioning A Leapfrogged World. *Worldchanging*, 5 February 2005. http://www.worldchanging.com/archives/002202.html
2. http://www.smartmobs.com/
3. Bogle, B. (2006). Could mobile social networks be the next big thing? *MobileActive*, 25 June 2006. [http://mobileactive.org/could-mobile-social-networks-be-next-big-thing]
4. http://www.futurelab.org.uk/resources/publications-reports-articles/literature-reviews/Literature-Review203/
5. http://www.mobilemedia2007.net/
6. http://www.brandrepublic.com/bulletins/digital/article/588614/mobile
7. http://mmaglobal.com/main
8. http://www.marketingsherpa.com/cs/mobilecampaign/study.html
9. http://www.social-marketing.com/blog/2006/05/cell-ing-out-using-mobile-phones-for.html
10. http://www.sextextsf.org/
11. http://mlearning.edublogs.org/
12. http://www.mobileactive.org
13. http://captology.stanford.edu/notebook/
14. http://mobilepersuasion.com/
15. http://www.1ktv.com/

Mobile Health Applications: Turning Up the Volume

Mobile applications are on the verge of overtaking social network sites as the next BIG thing in the digital health world. The signals are coming through in many places. At the National Conference on Health Communications, Marketing and Media[1] there was a session dedicated to presentations about applications of mobile in public health in which I participated. Yet, in another session, the speaker tried to stress the mobile *bonafides* of a program that simply featured an actress using a mobile phone in a public service announcement – I don't even remember the health topic as I was too preoccupied with sorting out what having a cellphone in a PSA had to do with 'going mobile.' But clearly the perceived professional norm is to become engaged with this new media.

One example of a useful application of mobile is a HIV prevention campaign by the BBC World Service Trust[2] that is producing public service advertising to promote condom use in four states in India. The campaign strategy is based on their research finding that men who talk about sex are more likely to use condoms consistently. The objective is to get men talking about condoms. The PSA released this month does use a cellphone, but it is executed around how the ringtone goes off at a wedding with the chant of condoms, condoms and a SMS call-to-action to download it to your phone (entertaining to say the least).[3] At the campaign website people can also download the campaign ringtone and wallpaper - nice execution for a campaign designed to get men talking (and a reminder that mobile doesn't have to work in a communication silo – media multiplexity is important.[4] [thanx to Mobile Active[5] for that tip]

Then there are the calls I get to talk about this work. Though most of the program at the Digital Pharma conference[6] centers on social networks, Cheryl Ann Borne from Skyscape[7] and I will be doing a pre-conference workshop on *Using Mobile Technologies in Pharma Marketing Initiatives to Support Behavior Change in Key Stakeholders*. Also on my schedule in the next month for presentations on mobile applications in public health are the National Safety Council Congress & Expo[8] and the Illinois Public Health Institute Conference.[9] And though I won't be able to make it, MobileActive 08, a global summit on mobile technology for social impact to be held in Johannesburg looks like a great event.[10]

I also came across an announcement of the formation of a membership organization Center for Cell Phone Applications in Healthcare[11]. Among the benefits they list for mobile the technology:

- *Cell phone and smart phone users can store their personal health information safely and securely on their phone in order to share it with authorized healthcare professionals when healthcare services are needed.*
- *Specific software can provide preferred and easy communication between healthcare providers, patients, payers, pharmacists, and others, facilitating medication reminders for patients, appointment scheduling, easy emergency calling, and other functions.*
- *The cell phone can serve as the platform for consumer health-related software such as wellness-related programs and disease management programs. A wealth of functions related to diseases ranging from asthma to diabetes, from smoking cessation to general pediatric applications, are currently being developed and tested.*
- *Offering consumers health-related Internet access, cell phones can allow a patient to quickly and easily look up information about medications or symptoms of their health status. Imagine a patient looking up a specific medication after it has been prescribed at a clinic visit, noting it interacts with another of their medications that they failed to mention during their visit and alerting the clinic physician — also via the cell phone - before having the prescription filled.*
- *Cell phones can be very efficient tools for medical research, enabling patient data to be transmitted easily and instantaneously to authorized, pre-programmed research centers.*

This list might give the people planning and developing a national health information network some things to think about. And they don't even address the use of mobile technology for health promotion and disease management.

Plenty to think about and act on. If you work in a nonprofit organization and want to explore how you can set up your own text-based mobile applications for minimal costs (the basic software is free), then check out FrontlineSMS[12] and the Desktop SMS Campaign Tools[13] discussion.

Notes

1. http://www.cdc.gov/HealthMarketing/NCHCMM2008/
2. http://www.bbc.co.uk/worldservice/trust/news/2008/04/080805_news_india_condomcondom.shtml
3. http://www.bbc.co.uk/worldservice/trust/whatwedo/where/asia/india/2008/04/080806_india_gates_condomcondom_video.shtml
4. http://www.condomcondom.org/

5. http://www.mobileactive.org/
6. http://www.exlpharma.com/events/digital-pharma
7. http://www.skyscape.com/index/home.aspx
8. http://congress.nsc.org/nsc2008/public/mainhall. aspx?MMID=17&ID=17
9. http://www.iphionline.org/index.asp?Type=B_ BASIC&SEC={DCD30877-2A91-4646-834A-F6B4C415CD38}
10. http://mobileactive08.confabb.com/conferences/MobileActive08/ sessions
11. http://www.medrecinst.com/cellphone/index/html
12. http://www.frontlinesms.com/
13. http://mobileactive.org.wiki.desktop_SMS_campaign_tools

Going Mobile to Prevent and Manage Obesity

A recent review of mobile eHealth interventions for obesity ends with:

In their 2000 systematic review of mobile eHealth intervention studies, Revere and Dunbar concluded that "future studies need to identify which [eHealth intervention] models are best suited to which health behavior, whether certain delivery devices are more appropriate for different health behaviors, and how care can benefit from patients' use of portable devices". We conclude that the appropriate model for obesity and weight management is the tailored informational intervention modified according to design principles suggested by Social Cognitive Theory and the Social Marketing Model. The health behaviors to target are self-monitoring of diet and physical activity. The devices are Web-enabled "smart" cellular telephones and wireless PDAs. Given the lack of effectiveness of other interventions to prevent or treat obesity in a sustainable matter, trials of these persuasive, ubiquitous technologies are required without delay.[1]

For researchers and graduate students, social entrepreneurs and program designers, the mobile eHealth strategy may be a fruitful one to pursue both for research on how social marketing adds value to the use of these technologies and AS PART OF a comprehensive (see the 4Ps) obesity prevention program.

Note
1. Tufano, J.T., Karras, B.T. Mobile eHealth interventions for obesity: A timely opportunity to leverage convergence trends. *Journal of Medical Internet Research* [http://www.jmir.org/2005/5/e58/]

Mobile Experiences in Developing Countries

Two recent reports provide some data and experiences that can help you make the decision to go mobile and guide your planning for mobile health and social change interventions, whether you work in developed or developing world contexts. Both studies focus on the NGO sector so the feasibility and practicality issues are dealt with in a realistic manner.

"Rapid Assessment of Cell Phones for Development"[1] is a publication commissioned by UNICEF in South Africa to inform a strategy to launch a new generation of cell phone technologies to address development issues, particularly HIV/AIDS. The authors describe the project:

The long term objective of this activity is to support government and civil society programs to leverage partnerships with companies developing cell phone technologies and other related service providers to develop a comprehensive strategy and plan for monitoring treatment adherence, providing information on sexual health including help lines and services and prevention messages by the use of cell phone technology. The potential for harnessing the benefits of cell phone technology in other areas of concern such as gender based violence and violence and abuse against women and children is enormous. Potential, however, is mediated by factors that ensure the success of such initiatives — such as available infrastructure, contextual issues, resources, capacities and location of the project — both physical location and location within a larger project.

The study was done between December 2006 and April 2007 and looked at existing initiatives to deploy cell phone technologies for development and social goals. The mobile health and social change projects they profile in the report are:

- Mobile4Good (Kenya, Tanzania, Nigeria and Cameroon)
- Learning about Living OneWorld UK (Nigeria)
- South African Depression and Anxiety Group (SADAG)
- Dokoza Project (South Africa)
- MobilED (South Africa)
- Chipata Women's Mobile SMS project OneWorld Africa
- Xam Marsé SMS Market Information Service (Senegal)
- Maluleke Project (South Africa)
- Domestic Relations Bill Advocacy (Uganda)

- Women of Uganda Network (WOUGNET) Electronic Delivery of Agricultural Information to rural communities in Uganda
- Dunia Moja (Tanzania, South Africa, United States)
- Rwanda TRACnet HIV/AIDS Solution
- Phones-for-Health (PEPFAR supported countries)
- Connect Africa
- The Village Phone Initiative (Uganda and Rwanda, Cameroon, and the Philippines)
- The Network of Mobile Election Monitors (NMEM) Nigeria

"Wireless Technology for Social Change: Trends in Mobile Use by NGOs,"[2] published by the UN Foundation–Vodafone Group Foundation Partnership, reports on a survey conducted in December 2007 and January 2008 of 560 non-governmental organization (NGO) workers to uncover how they are using wireless technology to help reach various social, civil, economic, and political goals.

Among their major findings are:

Eight-six percent of NGO employees are using mobile technology in their work. *NGO representatives working on projects in Africa or Asia are more likely to be mobile technology users than their colleagues in areas with more 'wired' infrastructures.*

Ninety-nine percent of technology users characterize the impact of mobile technology as positive. Moreover, nearly a quarter describe this technology as "revolutionary" and another 31 percent say it would be difficult to do their jobs without it.

While **voice and text messaging are still the most common applications of mobile technology among NGO workers**, respondents report using wireless technology in a number of other ways, including photo and video (39 percent); data collection or transfer (28 percent); and multi-media messaging (27 percent). The survey also finds some NGO workers using mobile technology for more sophisticated purposes such as data analysis (8 percent), inventory management (8 percent), and mapping (10 percent).

The survey reveals that the **key benefits of mobile technology for all NGOs include time savings (95 percent);** the ability to quickly mobilize or organize individuals (91 percent); reaching audiences that were previously difficult or impossible to reach (74 percent); the ability to transmit data more quickly and accurately (67 percent); and the ability to gather data more quickly and accurately (59 percent). Not surprisingly, then, 76 percent of NGO users said they would likely increase their use of mobile technology in the future.

In-depth case studies are provided across a variety of topics and include:

• Delivering Patient HIV/AIDS Care (South Africa)
• Connecting Health Clinics and Remote Health Workers (Uganda)
• Lowering the Barriers for Access to Public Health Data (Kenya, Zambia)
• Connecting Youth to Sexual Health Information (United States)
• Delivering Food Aid to Iraqi Refugees (Syria)
• Facilitating Communication in Emergency Situations (Peru, Indonesia)
• Text Messaging as a Violence-Prevention Tool (Kenya)
• Text Messaging to Save Trees (Argentina)
• A Survey of Text Message 'Infolines' (South Africa, United Kingdom)
• Environmental Monitoring with Mobile Phones (Ghana)
• Protecting Wildlife and Human Wellbeing (Kenya)

Notes
1. http://www.unicef.org/southafrica/SAF_resources_cellphones 4dev.pdf
2. http://mobileactive.org/files/MobilizingSocialChange_full.pdf

The Cell Phone and Global Poverty

The cellphone's future in reducing global poverty, with the extra feature of following a user anthropologist search for clues to the next generation of cellphone design features [Jan Chipchase who also blogs at Future Perfect[1]], is the must read article in Sunday's *New York Times Magazine* (7 Apr 2008).[2] Many of the examples, and the reference to the report *The Next Four Billion*,[3] will not be new to regular readers. Yet, the article pulls together many threads to demonstrate the promise of what can happen when one shifts from thinking about a new technology to designing user experiences with it that help people become more productive.

Some of the statistics Sara Corbett compiles here focus the opportunity:

- It took 20 years for the first billion cellphones to be sold in the world; 4 years for the 2nd billion to be sold; 2 years for the 3rd.
- 80% of the world's population now lives within range of a cellular network.
- 68% of cellphone subscribers live in the developing world.
- For every additional 10 mobile phones per 100 people, a country's G.D.P. rises 0.5 percent.
- By microfinancing 'cellphone ladies,' Grameen Phone is now Bangladesh's largest telecom provider, with annual revenues of about $1 billion.

The nut of the article is in this observation: *the cellphone's ability to increase people's productivity and well-being, mostly because of the simple fact that they can be reached.*
...in an increasingly transitory world, the cellphone is becoming the one fixed piece of our identity. Having the cellphone number is the one way you can be located and connected 'just in time' to arrange anything from a meeting place with friends, to establishing the price of your crop or catch for that day before you get to the marketplace, to setting up a micro-enterprise cellphone business, to creating formal mobile banking services.

The article notes how text messaging is being used to send reminders to take tuberculosis medications in South Africa and for people to receive answers to questions they can pose anonymously about AIDS, breast cancer and STDs (and a note: there is a pilot project in Zambia using text messaging for follow-up with male circumcision patients and to conduct brief service satisfaction surveys).

Then there is the example during the recent post-election violence in Kenya that at one point saw the government send out this text message: *The Ministry of Internal Security urges you to please desist from sending or forwarding any S.M.S. that may cause public unrest. This may lead to your prosecution.* And to think at VA Tech they were only using email and white boards to alert students to a shooter on the campus!

Notes

1. http://janchipchase.com/
2. http://www.nytimes.com/glogin?URI=http://www.nytimes.com/2008/04/13/magazine/13anthropology-t.html&OQ=_rQ3D2Q26thQ26emcQ3Dth&OP=5085c542Q2F7u687Q5EyQ20Q7DQ22yynQ3A7Q3AQ7CQ7C_7Q7Cd7Q5Bc7hCeC.Sz67Q5BcCzn-Q5IQ22ykyYyeQ25EnQ26Q5InhY
3. http://www.wri.org/publication/the-next-4-billion

Mobile Access to the Internet

One third of all adult US users of the internet have accessed it wirelessly. The prevalence of wireless access through laptop computers, cell phones[1] and wireless-enabled PDAs[2] is the topic of the latest report from the Pew Internet and American Life Project.[3]

When compared to all other internet users, wireless connectors are more likely to be male, 18-49 years of age, Black or Hispanic, have a college+ education level and earn over $50K a year.

One quarter (25%) of all US adult internet users say they have a cell phone that connects to the internet with a wireless connection. One in eight (13%) internet users have a PDA that can connect to the internet using a wireless network.

Among internet users under 30 years old, 40% have cell phones that can access the internet and 17% have PDAs that can connect to the internet.

Among 30-49 year olds, 15% have a wireless-enabled PDA that they use.

Just a note to underscore the point that the prevalence of having a cell phone to access the internet is nearly doubled that of PDAs. Unfortunately, the report did not include the data for other age groups though I expect the difference is not as pronounced - yet.

The adoption of mobile technologies that can access the resources of the web is now hovering around the magical 25% number that may signal a tipping point for the entire US adult population.

Notes
1. http://en.wikipedia.org/wiki/Mobile_phone#Health_impacts
2. http://en.wikipedia.org/wiki/Personal_digital_assistant
3. http://www.pewinternet.org/pdfs/PIP_wireless.use.pdf

A Manager's POV

McDonald's Secrets of Success

After years of neglect, attacks from various outside groups, and tactical shifts of one sort or another, McDonald's has just returned it's 55th month of increases in global same-store sales. In a year when other stocks have been heading south, it is one of only two Dow Jones Index stocks whose value has risen. What has been the secret behind their renewed success? Andrew Martin takes a behind-the-scenes look in The New York Times[1] and finds it:

"Plan to Win," that barely fits on a single sheet of paper — a text that is treated as sacred inside the company. It lays out where McDonald's wants to be and how it plans to get there, all of this revolving around the "five P's": people, products, place, price and promotion [The 5th P (People) is usually added in marketing service industries where client or patient contact is a crucial element for success.]

What? you ask. The usual marketing mix? Yes, it seems that even the corporate world forgets where it comes from. The noteworthy idea here for social marketers and policy makers is that it is a great case study of what happens when a company - or your organization or agency - rediscovers marketing or applies it for the first time.

Here is their plan to win (from the 2006 McDonald's Canada Social Responsibility report[2]). Note how it is not just a set of statements, but also one of ownership (responsibilities for making it happen).

People - Our well-trained people will proudly provide friendly, accurate and fast service that delights our customers. We have a responsibility to maintain an inclusive work environment where everyone feels valued and accepted, to provide training and other opportunities for personal and professional growth, and to promote job satisfaction.

Product - We will serve food and beverages people prefer to enjoy regularly. We have a responsibility to give our customers quality product choices and to partner with suppliers that operate ethically and meet our high standards of social responsibility.

Place - Our restaurants and Drive-Thrus will be clean, relevant and inviting to the customers of today and tomorrow. We have a responsibility to manage our business in an environmentally-friendly way and to constantly seek ways to make a difference in the community.

Price - We will be the most efficient provider so that we can be the best value to the most people. We have a responsibility to maintain our values and high standards as we provide food that is affordable to a wide range of customers.

Promotion - All of our marketing and communications will be relevant to our customers and build our brand. We have a responsibility to maintain and build trust with all our stakeholders by ensuring that our marketing and communications efforts are truthful and appropriate.

Whether you are new to social marketing, or an old hand at it, consider whether you could put your organizational or agency marketing plan into a one-page sacred text.

Notes
1. http://www.nytimes.com/glogin?URI=http://www.nytimes.com/2009/01/11/business/11burger.html&OQ=_rQ3D2Q26sqQ3DmcdonaldsQ26stQ3DcseQ26scpQ3D2Q26page-wantedQ3Dall&OP=5d94e2eQ2Fs%288jszQ24Q5EVpQ24Q24Gusu BBKsBWsWWsjLVgP8VVsWWjLpe8pNQ22GFU
2. http://www.aboutmcdonalds.com/mcd/csr.html

Planning a Social Marketing Program

Developing a marketing plan explicitly, and implicitly, captures many of the core assumptions and understandings of social marketing. In its essence, a social marketing plan is a translation document (See: *What is a Social Marketing Plan?*) that distills...

1. Understanding of the epidemiology of the disease
2. The context in which the intervention is being planned
3. Organizational strengths and competencies
4. Partners' capabilities
5. Behavioral determinants
6. And audience insights

...into strategies and tactics that lead to positive impacts in health behaviors among priority audiences. What is included and excluded in it, how terms are defined, its implications for research and evaluation, how interventions are designed and resourced, and what it says as a statement for **'what is social marketing'** are taken quite seriously, and literally, by many (and I have been in more than several impassioned debates and discussions over the years on all of the above).

Phil Kotler and Nancy Lee have taken the lead on developing a model outline of a social marketing plan that they will present at the World Social Marketing Conference. The outline builds on the one presented in their book[1] along with their principles of success for social marketing programs that I have talked about before (See Post: *Principles for Success in Social Marketing*). This latest version was reviewed, and contributions to it made, by a larger group of social marketers including Alan Andreasen, Carol Bryant, Mike Newton-Ward, Michael Rothschild, Bill Smith and myself. This, I am told by Nancy, is the final version, and with her permission I am posting it below for you to review and hopefully adopt in your practice of social marketing.

Executive Summary
Brief summary highlighting plan, stakeholders, background, purpose, target audience, major marketing objectives and goals, desired positioning, marketing mix strategies (4Ps), and evaluation, budget, and implementation plans.

1.0   Background, Purpose and Focus
Who's the sponsor? Why are they doing this? What social issue and population will the plan focus on and why?

2.0   Situation Analysis

2.1   SWOT: Organizational Strengths & Weaknesses and Environmental Opportunities & Threats

2.2   Literature review and environmental scan of programs focusing on similar efforts: activities & lessons learned

3.0   Target Audience Profile (See Note #1 below regarding alternative terminology.)

3.1   Demographics, geographics, relevant behaviors (including risk), psychographics, social networks, community assets and stage of change (readiness to buy)

3.2   Size of target audience

4.0   Marketing Objectives and Goals

4.1   Campaign Objectives: specifying targeted behaviors and attitudes (knowledge and beliefs)

4.2   SMART Goals: Specific, Measurable, Achievable, Relevant, Time bound changes in behaviors and attitudes

5.0   Factors Influencing Adoption of the Behavior (See Note #2 below regarding the iterative process.)

5.1   Perceived barriers to targeted behavior

5.2   Potential benefits for targeted behavior

5.3   Competing behaviors/forces

5.4   Influence of important others

6.0   Positioning Statement
How do we want the target audience to see the targeted behavior and its benefits relative to alternative/preferred ones?

7.0   Marketing Mix Strategies (Using the 4Ps to Create, Communicate and Deliver Value for the Behavior.)

7.1   Product: Benefits from performing behaviors and any objects or services offered to assist adoption

- Core Product: Desired audience benefits promised in exchange for performing the targeted behavior
- Actual Product: Features of basic product (e.g., HIV/AIDS test, exercise, # daily fruits & vegetables)
- Augmented Product: Additional objects & services to help perform the behavior or increase appeal

7.2   Price: Costs that will be associated with adopting the behavior

- Costs: money, time, physical effort, psychological
- Price-Related Tactics to Reduce Costs: Monetary & Nonmonetary Incentives and Disincentives

7.3   Place: Making access convenient
Creating convenient opportunities to engage in the targeted behaviors and/or access products and services

7.4   Promotion: Persuasive communications highlighting product benefits, features, fair price and ease of access

- Messages
- Messengers
- Creative/Executional Strategy
- Media Channels & Promotional Items

8.0   Plan for Monitoring & Evaluation

8.1   Purpose and audience for monitoring and evaluation

8.2   What will be measured: inputs, outputs, outcomes (from Steps 4 & 6) and impact

8.3   How and when measures will be taken

9.0   Budget

9.1   Costs for implementing marketing plan, including additional research and monitoring/evaluation plan

9.2   Any anticipated incremental revenues, cost savings or partner contributions

10.0   Plan for Implementation and Campaign Management
Who will do what, when — including partners and their roles?

OF SPECIAL NOTE: (1) Alternative terms include: Target Market (the traditional term), Priority Market, Priority Audience. (2) The process is an iterative one. For example, you may need to revise objectives and goals after hearing of barriers and benefits in Step 5, or promotional ideas based on final budget realities in Step 9. (3) A separate plan will be needed for each target audience, even though part of one campaign. (4) Research will be needed to develop most steps, especially formative research for Steps 2-6 and pretesting for finalizing Step 7.

Note
1. Kotler, P. Lee, N. *Social Marketing: Influencing Behaviors for Good.* Thousand Oaks, CA: Sage Publications, 2008.

Principles for Success

The 2008 version of my social marketing class is ready to begin. Among the changes is adapting Phil Kotler and Nancy Lee's 3rd edition of *Social Marketing*[1] - subtitled now as *influencing behaviors for good*. In it, they list 15 principles for success. Here they are with some commentary.

Take advantage of prior and existing successful campaigns. They are referring to an environmental scan of campaigns, and applying lessons from them to your own. Unfortunately, few accessible descriptions of successful campaigns tell the real story about how they got to that point; that's usually where the lessons are. When you are doing this, focus on campaigns that are focused on your priority audiences, NOT the health issue. That's when you learn and possibly get some audience insights (See *Aspiring to Audience Insights – Part II*).

Start with target markets most ready for action. Almost every behavior change approach will echo this sentiment, and it is a correct one. Yet you also need to focus on the audience critical to the success of your program (See *Segmentation: The First Critical Decision*). And please stop referring to them as targets. If you respect their dignity and ability to make choices they might be less inclined to try and dodge your messages.

Promote single, simple, doable behaviors - one at a time. Again, a basic principle of any effort to change the behavior of an individual. But what model do you use when you are trying to change the behavior or hundreds, thousands or millions of people? And be sure to avoid preaching the public healthy behavior and focus on what's relevant to them.

Identify and remove barriers to behavior change. This approach to social marketing may have it's time and place, but it is less frequent than advice like this would lead you to practice. I'll quote myself here: *Addressing deficits and moaning about barriers seems to be in the DNA of too many public health programs; practice some positive deviancy and test whether building on aspirations and assets doesn't suggest different strategies and approaches. If nothing else, you'll have a more diverse collection of concepts to test with your audiences and partners* (See: *Five Suggestions to Improve Your Social Marketing Program*).

Bring real benefits into the present. Another well-known principle of behavior change dating back to at least B.F. Skinner and operant conditioning - though the authors prefer to attribute it to economic theory. Also realize that the benefits don't have to be shouted out for the audience to understand and respond to them (See: *Coming this Fall: Healthier Snacks for School Kids*).

Highlight costs of competing behaviors. See also operant conditioning where the size of the consequence (or vicarious exposure to, or expectations of, positive consequences if you want to flip to social cognitive theory) is a major determinant of whether a behavior is acquired. I wonder how many people practicing social marketing really understand the essentials of behavior change rather than making it so complicated? My impression is that they get too wrapped up in cognitive activities (intentions, beliefs, attitudes) and economists' guesses (and *Freakonomics* may not explain things that well either[2]) when the basics might be easier. And some behaviors may be more determined by social factors than they first appear (See: *Maybe IT IS All About Social Networks*).

Promote a tangible good or service to help target audiences perform the behavior. For international readers, this might seem to flip social marketing as generally understood on its head. For the social marketers in the developed world, a reminder that products are not just the 4Ps of pamphlets, posters, PSAs and publicity (See: *Health Communications, Social Marketing and Coke*). Strive for products and services that help people change and not merely be channels to inform or expose them to messages.

Consider nonmonetary incentives in the form of recognition and appreciation. I completely agree that monetary incentives are too often a default position for many change agents. Learning a little more about what motivates people is worth looking into.

Make access easy. For services and products, I agree. But social marketers also need to insure that their audiences have the opportunities to try new behaviors, practice them and then be able to sustain them (See: *When is it Social Marketing?*). Otherwise, behavior change is just an idea. This is where thinking about and targeting things, not people, such as environmental, structural and policy barriers makes sense.

Have a little fun with messages. They do point out that for some types of organizations even a little bit of fun might be out-of-bounds. But be careful not to make it a joke or have the fun overshadow the intent of the message ('I laughed so hard I didn't pay attention to what they were saying').

Use media channels at the point of decision making. Always a good strategy, though I prefer to think of this as just one of several openings (the right time, place and frame-of-mind) that we need to be present in. Research notes a person living in the US makes more than 200 decisions about food a day (See: *Designing How We Eat*). Those are plenty of openings to aim at for the obesity prevention folks.

Try for popular/entertainment media. Back to the 'make it fun idea' and entertainment education certainly can play a role in communication efforts - if you can get your audience to come and pay attention. But for scalable behavior change, I want to use media to reach an audience wherever they are and then worry about tone (See: *Going Mobile for Change*).

Get commitments and pledges. Another classic behavior management tool for individual behavior change that finds many applications are behavior contracts. A little more difficult to do for populations, but not impossible. And a nice way to begin to introduce price as incentives into the social marketing program (See: *Pricing as Market Strategy*).

Use prompts for sustainability. They are referring here to sustaining behavior, not the sustainability of social marketing programs (unfortunately). Their relentless focus on individual behavior change leaves a lot out of what concerns practitioners and policy makers.

Track results and make adjustments. Just be sure you are monitoring and evaluating the important things, not simply what is easy and measurable. Will you be able to answer the questions: So what? Who cares?

What we will continue to grapple with throughout the course, and indeed in the profession (or discipline), is how to use social marketing for scalable impact on health issues and not be bound by theories and approaches that try and do it one person at a time (See: *Scaling up HIV prevention programs – Step 2*). Been there, done that.

Notes
1. Kotler, P. Lee, N. *Social Marketing: Influencing Behaviors for Good.* Thousand Oaks, CA: Sage Publications, 2008.
2. Levitt, S.D., Dubner, S.J. *Freaknomics: A Rogue Economist Explores the Hidden Side of Everything.* New York: HarperCollins Publishers, 2005.

Making Theory Relevant – Part I

The comment I received from a student about the 'theory' class in social marketing (See: *Social Marketing Resonance with Students: Part I*) spoke for not only students, but I expect many professionals.

This was the first behavioral theory class that I have enjoyed in a very long time. While learning about the theories was repetitive, I felt like I learned a more useful way to apply them to interventions. This was a nice break from prior classes that examined behavioral theory. The other enjoyable aspect of this particular session is that we learned about theories that were developed recently... and not in the 1950's.

What is a given for most social marketing and health communications programs is that they are based on theories from long ago and/or far away from the topic at hand. When I have done research into what theories people use in public health programs, practitioners can describe (maybe) one or two, and academics describe their own (developing your own theory must be a prerequisite for tenure now).

That some authors want to impose a single theory on social marketers borders on malpractice.

People in the advertising and public relations worlds who work on social marketing projects don't even know what a theory is – unless they have been in the game for a while. They want you to believe that their past 'experiences' give them a better feel for what will work with an audience than any textbook. What they often fail to intuit is that these 'experiences' form their own naïve or folk psychological theories.[1] The difference between their theories and the ones in the textbooks is about several dozen to several thousand research studies validating them (and some will still argue 'what do the researchers know! I do this for a living!' Walk widely around them.).

Theories are helpful AND harmful for several reasons:

- Explains how or why things are related
- Guides you to what's important
- What questions to ask
- What you should do about it
- How you should measure success

In other words, the theory you use – whether old, new or personal – frames the way you look at a problem, try to understand it, go about solving it and attempt to measure it (for example, not one epidemiological survey has ever given me a clue about HOW to change risk behaviors, only that it needed to be done for certain population groups).

I was recently called into a family planning project at the beginning (thankfully) to help develop an overall approach and strategy. The initial discussion included something like 'We are going to use a theory-driven approach, you know, theory of reasoned action and stages of change, to enroll more women in our services.'' At one level I appreciated the nod to the conscious and deliberate use of theoretical models from the outset, but I also shuddered at the choices.
Let's take the first one today.

Nothing wrong with TRA[2], if you want to use a theory that even one of its originators has moved beyond. This is, what the student above referred to, as theory from the 1950s (well, not quite that long ago, but you get the idea). It is the canon for behavior change academics, one that must (?) be passed down to the graduate students of today for it's historical importance – although, unfortunately, most of those instructors I expect still believe it to be operational.

The integrative theory proposed by Fishbein & Yser, I will say from the outset, has its detractors in the academic realm, mostly, I gather, because it includes too much.

However, among the practitioners I have worked with, they find it a very useful and comprehensible road map for thinking about a variety of public health problems.

The integrative theory incorporates elements of three widely used theories in behavior change and communication interventions: the health belief model, social cognitive theory and theory of reasoned action. In this model, whether a specific behavior is performed depends upon (1) if one intends to engage in that behavior - which you can see depends on a whole lot of things, (2) if they have the requisite skills and abilities to perform the behavior, and (3) if there are no environmental constraints (broadly defined) to performing the behavior. Those are 3 pretty big IFs that research and social marketing efforts need to address.

Here's an example of how the model was used in the strategic planning document for the family planning program:

To improve the likelihood of engaging in family planning behaviors then, we must first look at what environmental constraints may be preventing women from engaging in them and act on those (or help people overcome them). Among the constraints identified in the audience research are the few facilities available in rural counties, busy clinic staff that makes local outreach and promotion efforts difficult, making time in their busy schedules for setting clinic appointments, and difficulties using the centralized referral service.

Second, we need to assess if the person has the necessary skills to access and effectively use family planning methods over time. Here we found that not understanding the eligibility criteria (due to confusing messaging and low literacy skills) and non-adherence with birth control methods over time (discontinuing pills or missing doses, reports of broken condoms leading to unwanted pregnancies) were the most common problems reported by research participants.

However, if the person does not have strong intentions to perform the behavior, we need to look at changing (1) attitudes towards performing the behavior, (2) perceived norms about performing the behavior, and/or (3) the person's perceived self-efficacy, or confidence in being able to perform the behavior.

Among the determinants of these intentions we found that conservative community values can play an important role in reducing conversations and public education activities around family planning. We heard few comments related to negative personal, peer or social attitudes towards their personally using birth control. Indeed, there were generally favorable attitudes about delaying pregnancy until the woman had graduated from school, had a steady job and boyfriend and otherwise was 'ready' to raise a child. We did not hear much about women believing they were not susceptible to becoming pregnant (though other research informs us that this is the most common reason from women to discontinue using contraceptives). There was also evidence that women do talk with each other about birth control, though no common times or places were discovered that might guide communication strategy.

Now some people will ask 'what about…?' And if you think that's an important variable to consider, first make sure your audience does too. While I am not going to defend this particular theory as all-encompassing (that is why there will be a second installment to this topic), what you can take away from this is: *the theory you use helps you to focus in thinking about the issue, asking relevant questions of your audience and forming program strategies that are both theoretically- and research-driven.*

Notes
1. http://en.wikipedia.org/wiki/Folk_psychology
2. http://en.wikipedia.org/wiki/Theory_of_reasoned_action

Making Theory Relevant – Part II

Unfortunately, the stages of change model[1] has become ubiquitous to many social marketing programs. First the disclaimer or bonafide: I was using this theory to develop the "Imagine Action" community physical activity campaign[2] many years ago – long before Alan Andreasen popularized it in his book[3] and since has been promulgated by others (including Kotler & Lee[4]) as THE social marketing theory. However, stages of change has been used, in my opinion, more often as a segmentation system (think of it as behavioral epidemiology, descriptive but not very helpful to change agents) than as the tool it was meant to be to select specific types of interventions to match people where they were in the stages of change process. And the notion that it is all about increasing the benefits and reducing the costs of engaging in a behavior is being waaay too simplistic. If people really acted that rationally we wouldn't need behavioral economics for example – not to mention several hundred theories of learning and behavior change.

What I talk with my students about is that all theories of behavior are initially developed to explain a particular type of problem. Originally, stages of change was an attempt to develop a typology of psychotherapies – that's why it is know formally as the 'transtheoretical model' (hmmm, social marketing as mass psychotherapy?). It quickly found utility and parsimony in working with addictive disorders – smoking cessation in particular, though over the years many of us have pushed its applications. The Health Belief Model, to pick on another frequently invoked theory among social marketing and health communications people, was developed to explain, predict and increase screening behaviors. Not that these humble beginnings should stop you from using them in other circumstances, but being mindful of their limits is important – and one reason why HBM in particular has spawned so many offshoots to explain other types of health behaviors.

So when a family planning program wants to use the stages of change model – why do I cringe? Well, because there is a better model specifically developed to address issues of family planning. And, here's the punch line, it looks remarkably similar to stages of change with one notable exception. It allows us to look at the social context of the behaviors. Indeed, it offers a very cogent, theoretical rationale for why we should be using social media to address family planning issues.

The Process of Behavior Change Framework proposes that people seeking or using family planning and reproductive health services move through a variety of intermediate steps, or stages, in the behavior change process. These stages are:

Preknowledgeable where they are unaware of the problems or their personal risk.

Knowledgeable in which people are aware of the problem and understand what the desired behaviors are (i.e., use of modern contraceptive methods).

Approving is the stage at which they personally are in favor of the desired behaviors.

Intending is the stage at which people personally express the desire to take the desired action.

Practicing or when people are actively using contraceptive methods.

Advocating is when people not only practice family planning methods, but advocate them to others. Once people reach this stage, they become effective change agents among their peers and within their social networks that, in turn, acts to reinforce their continuing to engage in contraceptive practices. That is, it is a strong predictor of people adhering to and not discontinuing their birth control practices.

For the family planning program, (See: *Making Theory Relevant – Part I*) this model allows us to think about and talk with people at each of these stages who may constitute distinct audiences or segments for our program, each requiring different methods and actions they can take that are relevant to their current situation with respect to using family planning methods. What is noteworthy here is the notion of the advocacy behaviors within one's social network as a behavioral maintenance strategy, a recruitment strategy and as a social media one. For us the obvious became: *how do we work with users to become advocates for family planning through their SNS and mobile tools and networks?*

That's a very different slant than just thinking about reducing environmental constraints, addressing intentions and improving skills. Let alone simply focusing on increasing benefits and reducing costs. One theoretical model is rarely enough in the complex world of learning new behaviors. Or as I leave my class:

- Theories should be tools – not straight jackets
- Theories can inform – and blind
- "The one with the biggest toolbox wins" – Frank Lawlis, one of my psychotherapy mentors
- "It's a complex world" – The Young Adults
- "There's nothing so practical as a good theory" – Kurt Lewin

Notes

1. http://www.uri.edu/research/cprc/TTM/summaryoverview.htm
2. http://www.ncbi.nlm.nih.gov/pubmed/10146803
3. Andreasen, AR. *Marketing Social Change: Changing Behavior to Promote Health, Social Development, and the Environment.* San Francisco: Jossey-Bass Publishers, 1995.
4. Kotler, P. Lee, N. *Social Marketing: Influencing Behaviors for Good.* Thousand Oaks, CA: Sage Publications, 2008.

Seven Rules of Projects

Most social markers and change agents work on projects – perhaps the least useful way to generate passion, commitment and results. Matthew May writes about The Seven Laws of Projects, and How to Break Them[1]. Worth a close look.

1. *A major project is never completed on time, within budget, or with the original team, and it never does exactly what it was supposed to.*

2. *Projects progress quickly until they become 85% complete. Then they remain 85% complete forever. Think of this as the Home Improvement Law.*

3. *When things appear to be going well, you've overlooked something. When things can't get worse, they will. (Murphy's Law says, "If something can go wrong, it will"—this is a corollary).*

4. *Project teams hate weekly progress reports because they so vividly manifest the lack of progress.*

5. *A carelessly planned project will take three times longer to complete than expected. A carefully planned project will only take twice as long as expected. Also, ten estimators will estimate the same work in ten different ways. And one estimator will estimate ten different ways at ten different times.*

6. *The greater the project's technical complexity, the less you need a technician to manage it.*

7. *If you have too few people on a project, they can't solve the problems . If you have too many, they create more problems than they can solve.*

OK, now that you know them – breaking them is the courageous next step. When has this worked for you?

Note
1. http://www.openforum.com/idea-hub/topics/the-world/article/the-seven-laws-of-projects-and-how-to-break-them-matthew-e-may

Brainstorming Tips

You know the feeling: it follows the announcement that 'we're having a brainstorming meeting.' Call it dread, dysphoria, or drudgery. What it isn't, and what has been beaten out of you and your colleagues or smothered in numerous previous sessions is enthusiasm, anticipation and a sense of 'anything is possible' when challenged by a brain-storming session.

If you're like me, you've been in too many sessions where the editing is fierce, the conversation is dominated by the leader/manager, most people are clearly self-censoring (that's if they are engaged at all) and, worst of all, you never see the results go anywhere. Bob Sutton writes up some tips for brain-storming[1] to pass around your office. Here's one:

A good brainstorming session is competitive—in the right way. In the best brainstorms, people feel pressure to show off what they know and how skilled they are at building on others' ideas. But people are also competitive in a paradoxical way. They "compete" to get everyone else to contribute, to make everyone feel like part of the group, and to treat everyone as collaborators toward a common goal. The worst thing a manager can do is set up the session as an "I win, you lose" game, in which ideas are explicitly rated, ranked, and rewarded.

We all pay homage to research and evidence bases for our work and audience insights to drive program development. But it is the creativity brain-storming can foster that inspires our staff, partners and audiences to do their best when engaging in social marketing and social change programs. Learn to unleash it.

Note
1. http://www.businessweek.com/innovate/content/jul2006/
   id20060726_517774.htm?chan=innovation_innovation+++design_
   innovation+and+design+lead

A Little Extra Push

For all the management books that are out there, I ran across this post on The Engaging Brand[1] that covered a lot of the little steps. Great list!

Imagine if you did these 10 things just one more time during each day.

1. *Just said one more thank you.*
2. *Just made one more visit to the team to encourage.*
3. *Just had one more idea*
4. *Just said "Have a go" one more time.*
5. *Just made one more coaching session to your team.*
6. *Just smiled one more time.*
7. *Just asked for feedback one more time.*
8. *Just asked how people were feeling one more time*
9. *Just told one more story of what success will look like!*
10. *Just tried one more time*

Who knows, maybe it will change your world - or somebody else's.

Note

1. http://theengagingbrand.typepad.com/the_engaging_brand_/2007/06/10_just_one_mor.html

Five Suggestions to Improve
Your Social Marketing Program

Over the past month I have had the pleasure of working with small groups that compose a national 'whole' for social marketing and health promotion. In three different workshops I was struck by how certain themes emerged with each group as we talked about social marketing and their future work. Here are a few thoughts for you to consider.

1. **Focus on your real audiences – not the ones you imagine you should.** Planners look outside of themselves, organizations and practice communities (partners, collaborators) when thinking about their audience – who often seem associated with the idea of 'people we can do something to/for.' The labels are 'people at risk,' 'disenfranchised,' 'underserved,' various combinations of demographics – you get the picture. Media representatives, policy makers, CEOs, partner organizations are NEVER on the list, even though they are often the people most critical to the success of the program. (See: *Segmentation: The First Critical Decision*) Overlooking who's critical to success is the blind spot in virtually every program I have ever looked at closely (not just what's in the journal article or presentation). They should be a priority audience and when we start talking about them like that, ideas for improving the social marketing program become obvious. Coca-Cola, for example, does not leave distribution to chance.

2. **Your brand is what they say it is.** The fallacy that your organization or group can control the world (even a small communication slice of it - at least in open societies) reaches into the very ways 'brand' is thought about and practiced. Too many people believe that a brand is something that can be created and projected as some monolithic entity, impervious to the realities of the world, our audiences and the marketplaces of conversation. Understanding that the people formerly know as the audience[1] actually control (yes, control!) your brand is the insight that leads to the action steps we got to in each workshop: focus on identifying, collecting and encouraging the stories people tell about us; not creating the messages we want to tell them.

3. **You can't do it alone.** Partnerships and collaborations are among the rhetorical nirvana of public health and social change. Yet the care and feeding of these partners and collaborators is absent in most cases – remember, they aren't typically a priority audience. As in #2, once we shift that thinking, each workshop ended with a next step of developing, strengthening

or weaving together their networks of partners. Of course, having the wisdom and resources to do this well (rather than simply being mandated by funders) is another set of questions (See: *Stifling Innovation in Community Coalitions and Networks* & *The Ideology of Partnerships*).

4.   **Clarity and Focus.** Our discussions of objectives also led to the recurrent theme that planners don't spend enough time focusing on behaviors to change. They tend toward lofty, abstract concepts or semantic deconstruction of what a 'goal' and an 'objective' really are – both of which are equally effective in sucking the passion out of the staff and the project. One of my quirks is to push groups into defining and refining their objective for each priority audience until I can see the audience doing it (translation: even an 'outsider' gets the picture). Once you can see people doing something new (and also remember that people change, not policies and organizations), it becomes easier to establish the marketing mix that encourages and enables people to achieve it.

5.   **It's all about aspirations and assets, not barriers and deficits.** There is a pervasive and largely unchallenged tendency among public health people to focus on 'meeting needs' and addressing 'barriers' rather than getting on to the business of improving health. I consistently note that public health people LOVE to talk about barriers, often for hours if you let them, because it's so…paralyzing. I suggest you consider the flip side: the aspirations of your audiences (See: *Aspiring to Audience Insights – Part A*) and collaborators and the assets they, your organization and community possess that can be leveraged for success. Addressing deficits and moaning about barriers seems to be in the DNA of too many public health programs; practice some positive deviancy and test whether building on aspirations and assets doesn't suggest different strategies and approaches. If nothing else, you'll have a more diverse collection of concepts to test with your audiences and partners.

Note

1.   http://journalism.nyu.edu/pubzone/weblogs/pressthink/2006/06/27/ppl_frmr.html

Benchmarking Social Marketing Programs

A new survey from the Association of National Advertisers[1] reveals that many commercial marketers face the same problems as social marketers when trying to construct and deliver integrated marketing programs.

- *Sixty-three percent of marketers rank organizational issues as the greatest challenge to successfully integrating their marketing efforts. More specifically, they identified the existence of "functional silos" inside their companies as a key challenge.*
- *Most marketers (72 percent) feel the development of the "Big" creative idea that can be leveraged across all marketing channels is the most important contribution an agency can make toward an integrated marketing campaign.*
- *Almost 50 percent of marketers want their agencies to be media neutral when developing an integrated marketing program.*
- *Sales data and ROI analysis are viewed as the most important measures of the effectiveness of an IMC campaign.*

So for the social change agents who look to the commercial sector for some inputs and points of comparison for benchmarking marketing practices:

- Intraorganizational and other management concerns are among the greatest impediments to successful marketing efforts: a fact that is rarely recognized in discussions of 'what goes wrong' with social change efforts.
- The work to gain the audience insight that leads to the 'big' idea is one of the more unappreciated elements of the 'great' or most successful social marketing programs.
- Truly inspired and effective campaigns do not come out of workbooks or by following 'recipes' (See: *Aspiring to Audience Insights – Part A*).
- Programs designed from a tactical communications (promotion or media) perspective rather than a strategic and comprehensive marketing one have less value in the short and long-term.
- The focus of marketing and change efforts needs to be on objective measures of change - not the feelings and perceptions of program and agency managers, stakeholders, informants or focus group participants.

Note
1. http://www.ana.net/news/2006/06_09.htm

Working Together to Do Good

Partnerships between public, voluntary and private sector organizations are the Holy Grail for social marketers. In practice, these types of partnerships exist more on paper than in action. While leaders in all three sectors set rhetorical priorities for working more effectively with each other, the mechanics of establishing and sustaining them can be more trouble than they seem to be worth. How to address some of these concerns and enable partnerships to achieve the desired outcomes were the themes of the last Innovations in Social Marketing conference. The proceedings of the conference appear in the Fall-Winter 2005 issue of *Social Marketing Quarterly*.

In his overview of the conference, Greg Niblett noted the importance of partnerships in virtually all social marketing projects whether they have environmental and policy change as their intended outcome or the implementation of programs aimed at specific behaviors of priority audiences/consumer groups. Key resources and infrastructure that exist in the commercial sector, and are often lacking in the social marketing sphere (and motivate agencies sponsoring social marketing programs to seek them out), include the lack of a sales force, established distribution channels, pricing history, a legacy of promotional successes, research and development, and manufacturing capacity. The intent of 'partnership development' is to establish a structure to achieve outcomes for each organization they could not reach on their own. Yet, Greg pointed out "In reality, it is a term that is used to finesse power differences and soften the difficult reality of subordinate relations."

Several of the presenters focused on an analysis of the exchange relationship between partners. The immediate need is to determine how engaging with partners fits with each organization's business or operational mission and strategy. Next is usually to determine what are the mutually rewarding benefits for all parties that can be supported with specific objectives and accountability standards, the 'right' business and financial arrangement (this can be complicated by constraints placed on public sector agencies who also regulate industry sectors and also cannot commit to exclusive relationships with corporations), and a shared understanding of the 'why are we in this together' and 'for how long' contours of the effort.

Representatives from all three sectors examined what each brought to the partnership dance. High visibility in the market place and/or among specific priority audiences, high credibility among influencers and other intermediaries and access to resources are the most important assets each partner has in the beginning of the partnership. The exercise of due diligence by all parties centers around how involvement in the partnership may negatively impact these three assets as well as their relationships with audiences, advocacy groups, regulators, stakeholders and other organizations (peers, competitors, partners in other projects).

Mona Grieser ended one of the sessions with a short list of recommendations that I've paraphrased here as Pointers for Partnerships.

- Invite everyone in the system to the initial discussions.
- Let them talk about their view of the world as it relates to the issue at hand.
- Find the common ground.
- Explore a common future.
- Dance with the people you trust not to step on your toes or otherwise embarrass you (not necessarily the ones who are the best at what they do).

What is interesting to me about the discussions at the conference, as represented in the proceedings, is that there is a lot of time given to roles, taxonomies, and the vetting of 'who is acceptable and who is not' as a partner. The actual management of this process received much less attention. Jim Mintz, formerly at Health Canada, included in his keys for success (1) assigning clear roles and responsibilities, (2) providing publicity for each partner on their contributions, (3) having an approval and verification process for all products and activities, and (4) providing for timeliness and quality assurance. One of his comments, having capable and experienced staff representing each partner may be the most important contributor to success. What the qualities and competencies are of these successful partnership managers is the unanswered question.

Interorganizational Relations Theory notes that organizations make decisions about whether to enter collaborative relations with other organizations based essentially on a cost-benefit, or exchange, model. Clearly, having mutual goals, similar interests and values, and norms that favor collaborative enterprises are also part of the mix that need to be considered in creating partnerships and moving from so-called "obligational" networks to more "action or promotional" ones to ultimately "systemic" or long-term ones.

The Ideology of Partnerships

RFPs for improving public health and social conditions are loaded with references to 'coalitions,' 'partnerships,' and other forms of interorganizational collaboration – often as preconditions to either submitting a proposal or in carrying-out the work. Francie Ostrower pleads for 'greater realism about partnering's benefits and limitations' in <u>Stanford Social Innovation Review</u>[1].

Ostrower reports the results of a program designed to encourage partnerships among community-based arts and humanities organizations to help them expand their audiences. As a condition for funding, local foundations either required or strongly encouraged CBO applicants to form partnerships. In interviews with staff from both the foundations and grantees, the investigators found that both groups recognized the positive benefits of partnerships: build organizational capacity, horizons and growth; expand and diversify audiences; and expand organizational networks (build social capital). However, they diverged as funders argued that partnerships increase efficiency by discouraging duplication and encouraging the pooling of resources. Grant recipients, on the other hand, noted the time-consuming and costly work of making the partnerships work (relationship building across organizations, logistical management such as scheduling and attending meetings); asymmetrical responsibilities among partner organizations where large ones spread responsibilities across multiple staff while smaller ones have to concentrate them on just one or two people; and the perceived inequities about roles, responsibilities and influence that lead to contention between partners.

Her analysis of the data pins the underlying problem as this:

Foundations seemed to encourage, and sometimes mandate, partnerships not necessarily because partnering was the best way to achieve a particular set of objectives, given a specific context and problem, but because partnering fulfilled the foundations' view of how the social sector should operate. Evidence of an ideological commitment to partnerships surfaced time and again in our interviews.

The outcome of this type of commitment is that grantees focus more on making the partnership work [ie., behaving as they are 'suppose to'] than on achieving the original objectives. Indeed, many grantees said that they would not have formed a partnership had it not been a requirement for obtaining the grant. My favorite quote: *...policymakers continue to heed a 'siren call of coordination remedies' because of coordination's value as a symbol that 'epitomizes widely shared social values or rationality, comprehensiveness, and efficiency.'*

The two major conclusions of the study are:

- *Assuming that a particular goal warrants forming a partnership...provide planning grants to give potential partners the time and incentive to explore more fully the feasibility and the costs of partnering.*
- *To ensure the success of a partnership, foundations must be willing to cover administrative costs and, in the case of large projects, they may need to consider funding a partnership manager.*

While the study focused on local foundations and CBOs engaged in a specific task, the contours of the problem are embodied in many other contexts. The bottom-line is not to allow the indulgence of ideological biases to take focus, time and energy away from the purpose of the work.

Note

1. http://www.ssireview.com/pdf/2005SP_feature_ostrower.pdf

Stifling Innovation in Coalitions and Networks

Highly linked and centralized coalitions are less likely to adopt new evidence-based public health programs than ones that are less dense and have more decentralized structures. That is the conclusion of a study reported by Tom Valente and colleagues that appeared in *American Journal of Public Health*.[1]

These important findings fly in the face of conventional wisdom that expects the adoption of new practices to be greater among dense coalitions than among sparse, or loosely connected, ones, and among ones with a strong central agency. In other words, tightly knit, hierarchical coalitions (think of the 'usual cast of characters' with a lead agency), and efforts to create and manage them, only reinforce the boxes they think and act in – aka groupthink[2].

The results are based on a study involving 24 communities targeted for interventions to promote the adoption of substance abuse prevention programs. In interpreting their data, the authors conclude: *our results suggest that simply increasing network communication or connectedness, or both, among coalition members will not result in improved adoption of evidenced-based practices.*

The findings should resonate with readers who work with diffusion of innovations models and serve as a wake-up call for the numerous funders and policy makers who insist on following an ideology of coalition and partnership development (See: *Ideology of Partnerships*) that rarely has theoretical, practical or empirical support.

I'll let the author's words explain the rest:

Communities that are less dense may have weak ties to other organizations that provide access to resources and power, which can be mobilized to adopt evidence-based practices. Too much density indicates that connections are directed within the group and do not provide sufficient pathways for information and behaviors to come from outside the group. Too much density leaves a coalition ineffective at mobilizing the resources it needs to adopt evidence-based prevention programs...

The main finding from our study is that <u>we should not assume increased communication in the form of network density will always benefit coalition functioning</u>. In this case, it was associated with decreased ability to adopt evidence-based programs. <u>System-level thinking and measures helped</u>

us reexamine naïve expectations about how community coalitions function and how to improve their capacity for the adoption of programs that work. [emphasis added]

Hopefully, it may help you and your colleagues reexamine some of your own assumptions about gathering for the common good.

Notes
1. http://ajph.aphapublications.org/cgi/content/abstract/97/5/880
2. http://en.wikipedia.org/wiki/Group_think

Upstream Social Responsibility

Corporate social responsibility programs have been labeled as 'doing good to look good' and nothing more than 'a placebo.' These more critical looks at what constitutes socially responsible business practices were the subject of one of my posts and another one I chose to feature as part of my first anniversary of blogging. (See: *Wherefore Corporate Social Responsibility*)

Six principles for corporate redesign to imbue social responsibility throughout the life cycle and operations of a company.

1. *The purpose of the corporation is to harness private interests in service to the public interest.*

2. *Corporations shall accrue fair returns for shareholders, but not at the expense of the legitimate interests of other stakeholders.*

3. *Corporations shall operate sustainably, meeting the needs of the present generation without compromising the ability of future generations to meet their needs.*

4. *Corporations shall distribute their wealth equitably among those who contribute to its creation.*

5. *Corporations shall be governed in a manner that is participatory, transparent, ethical, and accountable.*

6. *Corporations shall not infringe on the right of natural persons to govern themselves, nor infringe on other universal human rights.*

Daniel Yankelovich, in his keynote address to the 2005 Innovations in Social Marketing Conference, also challenged social marketers to reset their sights when working with the private sector on CSR programs.

The goal of social marketing should be to accelerate the promotion of ethical standards - stewardship ethics, the company's credo (why we do what we do in [sic] context of civil society values), and corporate social responsibility efforts - as the primary drivers behind business goals, targets, decisions, and actions.

Sometimes in our efforts to increase partnership efforts with the private sector that rely on using the downstream model (that is, focus on changing individual behaviors) we may be keeping other things the same.

Learn from P&G

I was tuned into Proctor & Gamble's new values-based strategy *to touch and improve more consumer's lives in more parts of the world... more completely* via @GrahamHill on Twitter (my social source of news) and his RT of the link to Rosabeth Moss Kanter's blog post[1].

We will provide branded products of superior quality and value that improve the lives of the world's consumers, now and generations to come. As a result, consumers will reward us with leadership sales, profit and value creations, allowing our people, our shareholders, and the communities in which we live and work to prosper.

While many people in social marketing and public health often look to companies such as Apple, Coca-Cola, McDonald's and Nike as models for successful consumer marketing to aspire to, P&G stands out among the best and most innovative. What is most attractive to me about P&G is that they have 10 different business areas, ranging from baby care to home care, with 43 brands of over a half billion USD each. If you are in the public health business - not just the obesity, physical activity, breast cancer, HIV prevention or tobacco control business - then the way P&G creates and manages a portfolio of brands, not a unitary one, is where you should go to school.

Here are a few nuggets quoted from their annual report – the core strengths to win[2]:

1. No company in the world has invested more in consumer and market research than P&G. We interact with more than five million consumers each year in nearly 60 countries around the world. We conduct over 15,000 research studies every year. We invest more than $350 million a year in consumer understanding. This results in insights that tell us where the innovation opportunities are and how to serve and communicate with consumers.

2. P&G is the innovation leader in our industry. Virtually all the organic sales growth we've delivered in the past nine years has come from new brands and new or improved product innovation. We continually strengthen our innovation capability and pipeline by investing two times more, on average, than our major competitors. In addition, we multiply our internal innovation capability with a global network of innovation partners outside P&G. More than half of all

product innovation coming from P&G today includes at least one major component from an external partner.

3. P&G is the brand-building leader of our industry. We've built the strongest portfolio of brands in the industry with 23 billion-dollar brands and 20 half-billion-dollar brands. These 43 brands account for 85% of sales and more than 90% of profit. Twelve of the billion-dollar brands are the #1 global market share leaders of their categories. The majority of the balance are #2.

4. We've established industry-leading go-to-market capabilities. P&G is consistently ranked by leading retailers in industry surveys as a preferred supplier and as the industry leader in a wide range of capabilities including clearest company strategy, brands most important to retailers, strong business fundamentals and innovative marketing programs.

5. Over the decades, we have also established significant scale advantages as a total company and in individual categories, countries and retail channels. P&G's scale advantage is driven as much by knowledge sharing, common systems and processes, and best practices as it is by size and scope.

6. P&G has earned a reputation as one of the world's best companies for leaders. We work hard at leadership development because, as a build-from-within company, our future success is entirely dependent on the ongoing strength of our talent pipeline.

Put another way:

Public health agencies should invest significant proportions of their resources in (1) talking with and understanding their audiences (rather than a few focus groups here and there), (2) innovating in public health programs (rather than recreating wheels or sitting still waiting for evidence bases to develop), (3) creating and sustaining strong public health program brands (not their corporate image), (4) being the go-to partner for public health retailers or intermediaries (not someone to avoid because of bureaucracy and painful 'processes'), (5) having in place common systems for getting things done across disease and behavioral risk areas (think about CDCynergy[3] for example), and (6) developing leaders rather than rewarding the status quo.

To sum it all up, as the new CEO Bob McDonald[2] phrases it:

I believe it comes down to one simple and remarkably constant factor: the clarity and constancy of P&G's Purpose. Since the Company was founded, we've been in the business of providing daily essentials that improve the quality of people's lives. We help people care for their babies, pets and homes. We make everyday chores easier to do. We help people look and feel better. We've stayed true to the inspiring Purpose of touching and improving people's lives in meaningful ways.

Perhaps McDonald's quote should be on the walls of the offices of more public health leaders - along with a strategy to win.

Notes
1. http://blogs.hbr.org/kanter/2009/09/fall-like-a-lehman-rise-like-a.html
2. http://annualreport.pg.com/annualreport2009/letter/strength.shtml
3. http://www.cdc.gov/healthmarketing/cdcynergy/editions.htm

The Costs of Fear

One of the intentions of my course on social marketing is getting students comfortable with the idea of creating experiences where we can learn, fail, and learn some more. The principle of learning from failure is designed not to overcome the fear of failure that many people believe is the source of all evil when it comes to innovations in organizations - and social marketing programs, but rather **the fear of criticism**. More great ideas are buried by fear of the devil's advocates and potential blamers than by any other source (See: *Facing Down the Devil's Advocate*). Failure is the easy part; it's dealing with all of the criticism (justified or not - see devil's advocate) that goes before it, during it, and long afterwards that sucks the energy, creativity and enthusiasm out of people, programs and ultimately your organization.

I was thinking about this problem again during a strategic planning workshop I participated in last week. How do you encourage, support and reward innovation in an organizational culture that, regardless of the rhetoric, is mired in risk aversion and the fear of criticism? I did not have any 'aha' moments during the meeting, but reading *Building a Values-Driven Organization*[1] on the plane led me to this section:

One technique we have developed to support the storyline of the 'compelling reasons for change' in an organization is to calculate the 'cost of fear' in an organization... For example, internal competition is rooted in fears concerning self-esteem. We compete rather than collaborate because we are more focused on self-interest than the common good... Empire building and information hoarding are motivated by similar needs. Hierarchy is rooted in fears concerning status and trust. Bureaucracy is rooted in fears concerning order and control...

The underlying fears in bureaucracy are 'things will fall apart if order is not maintained' and 'people will cheat the system if there are no controls'... The energy involved in 'doing' internal competition, bureaucracy, hierarchy, empire building, image, blame and information hoarding is not available for useful work. The effort and time that go into supporting these potentially limiting values result in a loss of productivity, efficiency, commitment, and opportunities.

Those are the costs of fear ... and I am not going to teach them. Why live them? And how do we change them?

Organizations don't change. People do!

Note

1. Barrett, R. *Building a Values-Driven Organization: A Whole System Approach to Cultural Transformation.* Burlington, MA: Elsevier, 2006.

Design Thinking

Making it Tangible

The on-going challenge for social marketers is turning intangible products (behaviors) and incentives/costs into relevant, everyday actions that have immediate and tangible consequences. The easy example is cigarette smoking, especially as we've gotten so good at it. Tobacco marketers had products in all sizes, shapes, nicotine and tar levels and brands. We had "no smoking" and "it causes _____(fill in the health problem)" that even graces the side of cigarette packaging today. Over time we realized that these exhortations and costs had little influence on teen smoking. We began to search for ways to package nonsmoking that wasn't just the default position of "not cool." We also needed more tangible and immediate costs and benefits (began focusing on bad breath and smells that turned off the opposite sex; being the rebel by not smoking).

The energy conservation folks have faced a similar problem over the years in my estimation. Yes, there are dozens of tips to conserve energy but those don't dial-in relevance or WIIFM for most people (that's What's In It For Me). Saving energy or money on the monthly energy bills, or reducing the rate of global warming are, I suspect, an even bigger stretch for most people than "getting lung cancer or having a heart attack in your 50s" or "spend your money on other things" are for a 15 year-old who is smoking cigarettes. Which is what makes this campaign from Sustainability Victoria[1] an eye-catcher. As noted at Duncan's TV Ad Land[2]:

"Every day, the energy consumed by the average Victorian home produces 654 balloons or 33 kilograms of greenhouse gas," Mr Theophanous said. "Research shows that people are concerned about climate change but don't necessarily think they can do much about it."

Making the intangible tangible; making the invisible visible. The insight the campaign can build on (See: *Aspiring to Audience Insights – Part B*): it's not that they don't think they can do anything, it's that they don't realize what they're already doing. Now if it were me: black balloon magnets and stickers for the kids to bring home from school and start putting on all the appliances. Think of them as point-of-choice or cues for action for all those tips we've been giving them.

Notes

1. http://www.saveenergy.vic.gov.au/
2. http://theinspirationroom.com/daily/2006/greenhouse-gas-in-black-balloons

Behavior Change Amidst Chaos

Most of our knowledge about changing behaviors comes from carefully designed and controlled studies that seek to, as much as possible, emulate the laboratory conditions and the scientific method[1] enshrined in the physical sciences. These approaches prided themselves on the objective scientist who carefully controlled all possible sources of variance and then systematically manipulated the level of one to detect its effect on an outcome (or dependent variable) of interest. What makes it science, and not delusion, is that the method can be replicated by other investigators and similar results are observed.

This reductionist model of science[2] has been the bedrock of public health science and social marketing for far too long. As the physical sciences challenged and moved on from conceptions of the world in which the whole is equal to the sum of its parts to one of complex systems[3], public health has also slowly embraced a guiding philosophy where the whole is greater than the sum of its parts – the social ecological model[4] being one attempt to become holistic. Yet, what fascinates me is what happens when meeting with experts who can spend hours mapping out all the elements, or co-determinants, of how and why children are not physically active and consume excessive amounts of calories. Then, gazing at a wall full of charts and figures showing these relationships, I ask the question: which one do we focus on to change? The answers that come back reflect the reductionist framework - which variables cause changes in another, the lack of data to support the primacy on one over another - and we invariably have more choices than resources to tackle them. *The trees have obscured the forest.*

A missing link in developing BIG change programs is not that we don't realize that change occurs in the context of larger systems, it is that **we do not know how to influence systems very well** - we have been acculturated to think about "A causes B that leads to C" (See: *Behavior Change Should Be HIV Prevention Strategy*). Or, Sources (or other characteristics) influence Messages sent through various Channels that lead to changes in Behavior among specific Audiences. One of the unsettling notions of the Web 2.0 world for reductionists is that Audiences become active agents in this process and the communication process becomes a system of inputs and feedback loops, not a simple progression of steps (that, if followed correctly, lead to 5% solutions at best – See: *Health Communication Campaigns: The 5% Solution*). These linear models of communication may be useful in thinking about some types of interpersonal (say patient-physician interactions) and mass communications (political campaigns). <u>In our social marketing and social change work we must step up and acknowledge that most of the behaviors we work with, and the circumstances in which we work with people, happen in a context of dynamic social networks and systems - both theirs and ours.</u> Understanding this context for influencing social change leads us to follow our colleagues in the physical sciences to consider chaos theory and complex adaptive systems as core ideas in our new approach.

Ken Resnicow & Scott Page explored some of the implications of this new thinking about chaos theory and complex adaptive systems for public health interventions[5]. Key principles they draw from these models are that:

<u>Behavior change is often a quantum event, rather than a linear and predictable one.</u> They cite as evidence to support this contention that almost half of all smokers who successfully quit report that it was the result of an unplanned attempt rather than a deliberate or progressive movement through stages of change. Likewise, drinkers who were non-problem drinkers at long-term follow-up were more likely to state that their decision to quit was the result of a transformational experience rather than a weighing of pros and cons or the encouragement of others to quit.

<u>Behavior change can resemble a chaotic process</u> in that it can be quite susceptible to initial conditions such as motivation or emotion, highly variable, and difficult to predict. The authors echo principles of health communication that call for reaching people when and where they are in the right frame-of-mind to be the most open and receptive to the message.[6]

<u>Change often occurs within a complex adaptive system</u> that involves multiple parts that interact in nonlinear ways and whose results are greater than their sum (e.g., cost, availability, legal restrictions).

As a result, public health interventions should place greater emphasis of the periodicity or frequency of interventions rather than their intensity. That is, as *providing opportunities for individuals to hit a motivational lever - not just more opportunities to engage in desired behaviors.* One empirical study supporting this view showed that exposure to multiple channels of a nutrition education program over a semester was the significant predictor of changes in nutrition knowledge and behavior, not individual components of the program.[7]

The practical implications of taking a more systems-oriented view for social marketers is that we have to rise above individual level determinants of individual behaviors (See: *Maybe IT IS All About Social Networks*). We have to understand how behaviors work in the ecology of the social and physical realities of our audiences - how are the current ones adaptive? What changes in the social ecosystem are necessary for new behaviors to be learned and practiced? How do we find the best combination of product, prices, places and promotions that work at multiple levels — individual, family and social networks, community, and the physical, economic and legal environments — to integrate into programs to improve individual and social welfare (See: *Social Marketing and Tobacco Control Policy*). For instance, how do we mix smoking cessation services with increased tobacco taxes, smoke-free workplaces and communication activities to achieve change, rather than argue over the merits of one approach over the other as reductionists are prone to do? And *how do we develop sustainable programs in which frequency of exposure over time becomes the process measure of choice for our programs, not reach?*

I am not suggesting here that you throw away all the old ways of thinking about the problems you tackle in your work - but examining them may help you reach some new insight or inspire a new program idea. Thinking about systems and your interventions can complement the way you construct social change (See: *Making Change Happen: The Marketing Approach*).

Notes

1. http://en.wikipedia.org/wiki/Scientific_method
2. http://en.wikipedia.org/wiki/Reductionism
3. http://en.wikipedia.org/wiki/Complex_system
4. http://en.wikipedia.org/wiki/Social_ecological_model
5. Resnicow K,. Page S.E. Embracing chaos and complexity: A quantum change for public health. *American Journal of Public Health*, 2007;**98**:1382-1389.
6. Sutton, S.M., Balch, G.I., Lefebvre, R.C. Strategic questions for consumer-based health communications. *Public Health Reports*, 1995;**110**:725–33.
7. Lefebvre, R.C., Olander, C., Levine, E. The impact of multiple channel delivery of nutrition messages on student knowledge, motivation and behavior: results from the Team Nutrition Pilot Study. *Social Marketing Quarterly*, 1999;**5**:90–8.

Walkable Neighborhoods:
It's More Than a Design Problem

Alex Steffen talks about an experiment of a colleague and his family to live a car-free lifestyle in Seattle.[1] While it was quite easy to identify a 1 mile perimeter 'walkshed' in which most of their daily activities occur, they identified a need for information tools (such as a map for their walkshed that locates area businesses and public facilities of various sorts) that would help guide their walking behavior. [Guess it beats wandering around aimlessly for at least 30 minutes a day most days of the week.]

Note
1. http://www.worldchanging.com/archives/004301.html

Designing How We Eat

One of the more popular trends in management and marketing is design thinking. While many people seem to toss this term around, Victor Lombardi[1] puts it pretty succinctly:

- **Collaborative**, *especially with others having different and complimentary experience, to generate better work and form agreement*
- **Abductive**, *inventing new options to find new and better solutions to new problems*
- **Experimental**, *building prototypes and posing hypotheses, testing them, and iterating this activity to find what works and what doesn't work to manage risk*
- **Personal**, *considering the unique context of each problem and the people involved*
- **Integrative**, *perceiving an entire system and its linkages*
- **Interpretive**, *devising how to frame the problem and judge the possible solutions*

Many of these points are shared with other approaches to problem-solving that take a person-centered approach and are sensitive to people's current context and realities. The feature that I like to stress is the experimental, or even playful, nature of the approach embodied in the philosophy of 'prototype it.' That is, rather than continue to argue and debate in the abstract what could be done to solve a problem, build it, test it, learn from it and move on. As Tom Peters is often quoted as writing: **Fail forward fast.**

More resources for learning about and applying design thinking include this article from *Business Week online*[2], many posts by Diego Rodriguez at *metacool* – start with this one[3], and Tim Brown of IDEO[4] in *Fast Company*.

All of this is prelude to the challenge: why aren't we applying design thinking more often to behavior change? For example, in the *New York Times*[5] -

"To a person, people will swear they aren't influenced by the size of a package or how much variety there is on a buffet or the fancy name on a can of beans, but they are," Dr. Wansink said. "Every time."

"We don't have any idea what the normal amount to eat is, so we look around for clues or signals," he said. "When all you see is that big portions of food cost less than small ones, it can be confusing."

Although people think they make 15 food decisions a day on average, his research shows the number is well over 200.

200 opportunities a day to influence what, and how, people eat?! I can remember when I first heard that the average family rotates about 10-12 recipes for dinner. The behavior design implication was obvious for promoting heart healthier eating patterns: change how they prepare those 10-12 meals.

If we could start understanding how people design (consciously or not) their eating patterns (funny that we call them patterns!), maybe more of these 200 opportunities would appear. And then we could start focusing on things like proximity and access to vending machines, product packaging and who we eat with.

The people at 30,000 feet can look down and say we need a wholesale change in our food system, in school lunches, in the way we farm." At the bottom of the pyramid, he said, are the nutritionists and the diet fanatics who think the problem will be solved by examining every nutrient and calorie.

There is a line of thinking in social marketing these days that 'upstream,' or 30,000 foot interventions, are where the action - and success - lie. However, I have yet to see a documented case where the air force won a war.

Designing behaviors - might it lead to some new ways of thinking about old and seemingly intractable problems?

Notes
1. http://noisebetweenstations.com/personal/weblogs/?page_id=1688
2. http://www.businessweek.com/magazine/content/06_41/b4004401.htm
3. http://metacool.typepad.com/metacool/2006/08/so_we_must_cons.html
4. http://www.fastcompany.com/magazine/95/design-strategy.html
5. http://www.nytimes.com/glogin?URI=http://www.nytimes.com/2006/10/11/dining/11snac.html&OQ=_rQ3D3Q26pagewantedQ3DIQ26thQ26emcQ3Dth&OP=6ebdf8f8Q2FQ20wQ60EQ20oLsQ7BQ27LL%29DQ20D99HQ20Q259Q20Q25Q25Q20oyvyvQ5BQ20Q25Q25Q7Bv@shQ7D%29gQ24

Can Behavior Change Become Popular?

It was a pleasure to find a popular book that begins and ends with the science of behavior change - social cognitive theory. Once I saw the first reference to Albert Bandura (the most cited psychologist alive), I hoped this book would be different from the usual story-telling fare. As a second generation Bandura progeny (in the academic world, my dissertation advisor and major professor, David Rimm, was one of "Uncle Al's" doctoral students and Dr Bandura kindly reviewed and commented on my dissertation proposal and results), I can say that my expectations were met.

Influencer: The Power to Change Anything[1] complements my recent post noting that it is skills in social marketing that are needed to help the new legion of change agents. The authors note ...*what most of us lack is not the courage to change things, but the skill to do so.* And that most of the wicked problems *don't require solutions that defy the laws of nature; they require people to act differently.*

The book draws on the work of several 'master influencers' and social cognitive theory to provide guidance to anyone who wants to be an influencer. While the vicarious experience (when was the last time I saw those words in print?) of reading the stories will be helpful to many, achieving success at scale with social marketing is not addressed here (guess you will have to stick with this blog a bit longer). What every social marketer and change agent will find here though are the basic principles for behavior change that should be the essence of your change vocabulary and actions:

- Finding high leverage behaviors (which behaviors are the most important ones to change) through the study of positive deviants. Is it possible, as the authors report, that exercising on home equipment, eating breakfast and weighing yourself daily are the vital behaviors for achieving at least 30 pound weight loss and keeping it off for at least 6 years? My look at their source, the National Weight Loss Registry[2] showed a more complicated picture, but still far from having to focus on over 200 eating decisions people make a day.
- Changing minds needs to focus on two, and only two, essential questions: Is it worth it (change outcome expectations)? and Can I do this (change self-efficacy)? That is, motivate and/or enable a vital behavior.

- Using three sources of influence on motivations and abilities - personal, social and structural - and connecting them to six behavior change strategies of (1) making new behaviors desirable, (2) surpassing personal limits, (3) harnessing peer pressure, (4) finding strength in numbers, (5) designing rewards and demanding accountability and (6) changing the environment.

In their discussion, the authors reinforce the need for us to become much more attentive to how our actions as change agents build social capital - and not just social support. They also address the 'environmental incompetence" of many change agents, not in the 'green' sense of the word, but in our failure to notice how often even minor modifications in the environment (the size of the cups that are offered in fast service restaurants and convenience stores) have profound impacts on behavior. They also offer additional tools and resources at a companion website you can check out as well.[3]

People from marketing backgrounds have promoted the transtheoretical (stages of change) model as the de facto theory of behavior change in social marketing (despite the fact that few get beyond using it as a segmentation scheme and trying to reduce perceived costs of change). But as someone who was educated and trained as a behavior change scientist, give me SCT any day for a robust and dynamic approach that incorporated structural and environmental change, modeling, diffusion, social norms and collective action long before many people rediscovered and began repackaging them. *Influencer* makes a good place to start expanding your approach to changing behaviors. Follow it up with health promotion from the perspective of SCT.[4] Then be a more effective social marketer.

Notes

1. Patterson, K., Grenny, J., Maxfield, D., McMillan, R., Switzler, A. *Influencer: The Power to Change Anything*. New York: McGraw-Hill, 2008.
2. http://www.nwcr.ws/Research/default.htm
3. http://www.vitalsmarts.com/influencer_book.aspx
4. Bandura, A. Health promotion from the perspective of social cognitive theory. *Psychology and Health*, 1998;**13**:623-649. [http://des.emory.edu/mfp/Bandura1998PH.pdf]

Social Models for Marketing: Diffusion

Among the most data-driven models for behavior change, particularly at scale or on a population-basis, is Rogers' diffusion of innovations. When I reviewed the most popular theories and models then being used in social marketing programs, I added that Diffusion of innovations research and concepts offer a tremendous amount of insight for social marketers to use in designing their programs, yet we see very little active discussion of it in social marketing circles.[1] Social diffusion offers one of the most robust theories for taking innovations in ideas, behaviors and practice to scale. Yet, though the calls for scaling up successful behavioral interventions for such things as HIV prevention are reverberating around the globe,[2] we see little discussion or application of the model by social marketers or, for that matter, few others in public health.

Social marketing needs to focus on 'pushing the curve' of adoption of health practices among individuals, the adoption of effective interventions among practitioners, and the adoption of health-promoting and supportive policies among policy-makers. Adopting diffusion of innovations means that we understand how and why people adopt (or fail to adopt) healthier, environmentally conscious or socially beneficial behaviors. These characteristics include (a) the contextual factors that surround the adoption of new practices and policies, (b) people's perceptions of the innovation as a normative behavior among their reference group or peers (which studies suggest account for anywhere from 50-86% of the variance in the rate of diffusion of new behaviors), and (c) a risk-benefit analysis that substitutes certainty of outcomes and familiarity with the new behavior over costs and benefits of changing current ones.[3]

Social marketers need to design their behavior, product and service offerings to answer the questions people have that are associated with adoption or termination:

- How is this better than what I currently do? ·
- How is it relevant to the way I go about my everyday life? ·
- Is it simple enough for me to do?·
- Can I try it first?
- Can I watch others and see what happens to them when they do it?

Social marketing for behavior change at scale also needs to explore more extensively the use of audience segments such as:

Innovators: who have a high tolerance of risk; are fascinated with novelty; usually viewed by others in their community as mavericks, not opinion leaders; and whose social networks transcend geographic boundaries.

Early Adopters: who are the community opinion leaders and well-connected socially and locally; have the resources and risk tolerance to try new things; and are the people who are watched by others – and they know it.

Early Majority: the people who are very engaged in local peer networks; rely on personal familiarity before adoption and continually ask the question 'How does this new behavior, product or service help me?'

Late Majority: the group of people who are most sensitive to peer pressure and norms, yet very cautious about change of any kind; they seek to minimize uncertainty of outcomes and want to see the proof of relative advantage locally – not read about it on web sites or see it on television.

Laggards: these are the traditionalists who believe in the tried and true; they are near isolates in their social networks which explains why they can be so difficult to reach and influence (versus having individual deficits); they are often suspicious of innovation and change agents; and they are seeking assurances that adoption of new behaviors (such as stopping smoking, driving a low carbon emission vehicle) will not fail.

The diffusion of innovations literature should also wake-up policy-makers and social marketers that there are immediate needs to apply marketing principles to such social goals such as improving evidence-based practices in public health and medicine. Maibach, Van Duyn & Bloodgood[4] suggest three marketing-based solutions: (1) conduct consumer research with prospective adopters to identify their perspectives on how evidence-based prevention programs can advance their organization's mission, (2) build sustainable distribution channels to promote and deliver evidence-based programs to prospective adopters, and (3) improve access to easily implemented programs that are consistent with evidence-based guidelines.

There are lessons we have learned over the years that can be used to re-conceptualize social marketing strategy to promote diffusion of product and service use as well as adoption of new behaviors.

1. Find sound innovations/solutions. Ones that meet the criteria noted earlier and are relevant to people's everyday lives.

2. Provide opportunities for Innovators to discover them.

3. Engage the curiosity of the Early Adopters.

4. Target the weak ties between Innovators and Early Adopters through identifying the 'boundary spanners' who interact with multiple networks.

5. Promote the work of Early Adopters.

6. Create spanable social distances between groups through various means including using social media such as social network sites and blogs and convening meetings of the 'unlike' rather than the usual host of agents.

7. Enhance the salience and attractiveness of the 'positive deviants' – the people who are already practicing the target behavior or using the product and service; put the practitioners of 'new' behaviors in contexts and situations that attracts imitation or modeling.

8. 'If you can't imitate them, don't copy them.' Expect and encourage reinvention.

9. Support time and energy for discovery, testing, networking, adapting, monitoring and preserving the past. Do not write off the traditionalists, especially when encouraging organizational change.

10. It starts with yourselves and your partners.

With respect to this last point, remember that highly linked and centralized coalitions are less likely to adopt new evidence-based public health programs than ones that are less dense and have more decentralized structures.[5] What is important for adopting new practices and programs are 'boundary spanners' or individuals from organizations who are not tightly bound exclusively to the clique (or usual cast of characters). These are the people more likely to be open to innovation; the traditionalists have their own, seemingly immutable, point-of-view.

Our challenge in the years ahead, whether it is in HIV prevention or the prevention of childhood obesity, is to apply in a deliberate and systematic way what we have learned from the evidence-base of diffusion research to achieve broad and sustainable change. It seems that very few policy-makers, behavioral change experts and public health officials know how to transform programs focused on individual behavior change to ones scaled for population impact. And few program directors and donors seem willing to take the risk that is inherent in moving from 'the zoo' of controlled experiments to 'the jungle' of people's real lives. Social marketing provides us with a framework to fill this gap between knowledge and practice.

Notes

1. Lefebvre, R.C. Theories and models in social marketing. In P.N. Bloom and G.T. Gundlach (eds), *Handbook of Marketing and Society*. Newbury Park, CA: Sage Publications, 2001 (pp. 506-5180.

2. Global HIV Prevention Working Group. (2007) Bringing HIV prevention to Scale: An urgent global priority. [http://globalhivprevention.org/pdfs/PWG-HIV_prevention_report_FINAL.pdf]

3. Rogers, E. *Diffusion of Innovations* (4th Ed). New York: The Free Press, 1995.

4. Maibach, E.W., Van Duyn, M.A., Bloodgood, B. A marketing perspective on disseminating evidence-based approaches to disease prevention and health promotion. *Preventing Chronic Disease* [serial online] July, 2006. [http://www.cdc.gov/pcd/issues/2006/jul/05_0154.htm]

5. Valente, T.W., Chou, C.P., Pentz, M.A. Community coalition networks as systems: Effects of network change on adoption of evidence-based prevention. *American Journal of Public Health*, 2007;**97**:880-886.

Design Thinking, Social Marketing and Behavior Change

Design thinking has been taking over the conversation about innovation in business, marketing and yes, design. Championed by organizations including IDEO and the Rotman School of Management, design thinking focuses on the process for practical, creative resolution of problems or issues with an improved future result. The future result might be a new or improved product or service, new processes or experiences for consumers or users, or new social and organizational systems.

Like social marketing, design thinking starts with a human-centered approach that enables us to collectively tackle problems and ideas that are more complex than the lone designer can imagine: inaccessible healthcare, billions of people living on a few dollars a day, energy usage outpacing the planet's ability to support it, education systems that fail students, and beyond. Familiar territory to social marketers and other kinds of social change agents. I think it's time for more design thinkers and social marketers to get to know each other and work more together, exchange ideas and bring innovation to wicked problems that desperately need our collective attention and for more design thinking to permeate into public health people's heads, hearts and actions. (See: *IDEO Questions for Social Marketers*).

I have been using design concepts for a couple of years now in various guises, notably in the adage of our need to pay more attention to the 'design of behaviors,' or behavioral design, in many of our programs. We also need to bring more design thinking into social marketing programs that focus on creating and delivering products and services as well. And in public health more broadly, design thinking may just be the additional stimulus to bring more people over to the idea that **our work is really about people, not audiences.**

For social designers and marketers (with apologies to the social designers who tend to focus on products to benefit society) who are aspiring to create experiences in which people can learn new things – and not be at the mercy of our trying to change their behavior – I put together a slide show to introduce the basic principles for how people learn. One of the takeaways I hope you get from this post is that there is a consequential aftermath of thinking about 'changing people's behavior' versus 'helping people learn new behaviors.' It all depends on whose POV you want to take. I would hope most designers and marketers would start shifting to the latter perspective. Understanding how people learn would make a great start. Let me know what you think!

IDEO Questions for Social Marketers

The 2007 Innovations in Social Marketing Conference theme was *It's All About the Customer* and among the presentations was *How Design Thinking and Innovation Can Influence Customer-Oriented Behavior Change Strategies* by Chris Waugh and Holly Kretschmar of IDEO. The best part of their presentation and the group exercise they conducted to demonstrate the IDEO approach was, for me, their <u>Nine Questions We've Been Asking About Social Marketing</u>:

1. What if we called ourselves story-tellers - what if we called them creators instead of consumers?
2. What if our brand was about helping people reach their goals?
3. What if a social change movement could be successful with little to no promotion?
4. What if we embraced experiments (or prototyping) instead of waiting for the perfect answer?
5. What if the people we served created the messages?
6. What if we invited people at the extremes to put our messages in surprising places?
7. What if people were clamoring to play with us?
8. What if we understood our stakeholders as well as we understand the people we serve?
9. What if social marketers were synonymous with trusted advisors?

Food for thought, and a way to start thinking about how to improve your own social marketing programs.

The Change We Need

Improving Public Health: What is Needed is More Social Marketing

The King's Fund calls for more innovation in public health approaches that have tended to focus only on information and communication campaigns (See: *Health Communications Campaigns: The 5% Solution*) or just offering financial incentives (See: *The Price of Change*). The report summarizes the results of a year long study[1] of the effectiveness of various types of public health interventions that address smoking, alcohol abuse, obesity and physical inactivity. The conclusions of Kicking Bad Habits[2] include:

- *The National Health Service (NHS) needs to make better use of social marketing techniques and data analysis tools like geodemographics to identify, target and effectively communicate messages and motivate people to change how they live.*
- *Public health programmes shouldn't rely on just one approach — such as information campaigns or financial incentives — as the evidence shows the most effective behaviour change interventions employ a variety of tactics.*
- *A robust evaluation — of short- and long-term changes in behaviour and health outcomes — should be made a requirement of all public health programmes in order to build an evidence base for the future.*
- *Frontline staff should be more proactive in promoting healthy habits to the patients they see every day and for contracts and incentives to be used to encourage such behaviour.*
- *Government departments and local agencies involved in tackling unhealthy behaviours must better co-ordinate their efforts and ensure that targets are agreed to support their shared objectives.*

My experience suggests that a similar study in the US would come to quite similar results. To fulfill the campaign promise of the Obama-Biden team to promote public health[3], they will need to look beyond their stated intentions to require coverage of preventive services, including cancer screenings, and increase state and local preparedness for terrorist attacks and natural disasters. The wicked problems[4] of tobacco use, obesity, physical inactivity, increasing rates of childhood diabetes and other public health issues - not to mention many of the social issues facing the country - require innovations in how we think about influencing behaviors at the individual and systems levels. Why not a similar high level review and clear statement of what really works here - one that extends beyond HHS to include Education, Environment, Commerce, Housing, State and Treasury? And will they take advantage of the current work on developing

Healthy People 2020 to bring change to public health priorities and practices in the next decade - not just domestically but in our global health efforts as well? I think it is time for a road map for public health promotion (not public health care) that is more than rhetorical priority and works in tandem with the health care activities that are already well underway during this transition time.[5]

Notes

1. Boyce, T., Robertson, R., Dixon, A. (2008). *Commissioning and behaviour change: Kicking Bad Habits final report.* The King's Fund.
2. http://www.kingsfund.org.uk/press/press_releases/
3. http://change.gov/agenda/health_care_agenda/
4. http://en.wikipedia.org/wiki/Wicked_problem
5. http://change.gov/page/s/hcdiscussion

How Do We Address Wicked Problems: The Australian POV

Wicked problems are all around us. They are defined in Wikipedia[1] as ones that are *difficult or impossible to solve because of incomplete, contradictory, and changing requirements that are often difficult to recognize. Moreover, because of complex interdependencies, the effort to solve one aspect of a wicked problem may reveal or create other problems.* Examples include what to do about climate change, health care, the HIV pandemic, flu preparedness, drug use, mental health care and obesity prevention.

I have written about how social marketing provides a complimentary approach to the more traditional public policy tools that are used to tackle these and many other types of social problems (See: *The Change We Need: New Ways of Thinking about Social Issues*). For another, independent point of view (POV), I have selected some of the summary comments from the Australian Public Service (APS) Commission's report[2] on *Changing Behavior: A Public Policy Perspective*. For those of you who work in and around policy-shapers and makers it makes several relevant points about the need to move away from outmoded and largely discredited 'rational choice' models to more comprehensive approaches in which social marketing can serve as a useful heuristic and integrating framework (for more about these people as market agents see: *The Policy Maker Audience*). Be sure to share this with them.

Governments regularly use a range of traditional policy tools to influence citizens' behaviour, including legislation, sanctions, regulations, taxes and subsidies, the provision of public services and information and guidance material. In many areas this range of traditional tools works well. For some social policy problems such as so-called wicked problems, however, influencing human behaviour is very complex and the effectiveness of traditional approaches may be limited without some additional tools and understanding of how to engage citizens in cooperative behavioural change. It has become increasingly clear that government cannot simply deliver key policy outcomes to a disengaged and passive public. In the areas of welfare, health, crime, employment, education and the environment, achieving significant progress requires changing behaviour.

Detailed cost-benefit analyses in a number of key areas of public policy such as health and crime have shown that more sophisticated behaviour-based interventions can be very much more cost-effective than traditional approaches to policy and service delivery. This is particularly the case if a longer-term time frame is taken to evaluate the constraints, costs and benefits. Agencies may have more impact on key policy outcomes by using their limited resources to more effectively engage, involve and change the behaviour of users and other parties, than by concentrating only on traditional policy tools and service delivery.

Accordingly, policy makers in the APS need to have a better understanding of how the rational choice model of behavioural change can be supplemented by insights from behavioural change theory and evidence at the individual, interpersonal and community levels. A social marketing approach is one practical tool that tries to integrate these three levels of theories.

. . . The need to formulate a comprehensive approach to behavioural change, to understand how components interact, to work cooperatively across jurisdictions and organisations and to engage stakeholders, highlights the need for a range of core skills in addition to the more traditional analytical, conceptual and project management skills. These include communication and influencing skills, the ability to work cooperatively, and big-picture thinking skills. There is also a need for policy makers to be aware of and apply behavioural change theory, and to understand the importance of investing in evaluation and research.

Notes
1. http://en.wikipedia.org/wiki/Wicked_problem
2. http://www.apsc.gov.au/publications07/changingbehaviour.pdf

Social Marketing, Hard Power, Soft Power and Social Change

"Today I want to make the case for social marketing becoming a core part of the public policy-making arsenal" was the beginning of a speech, <u>Getting the balance right: the role of soft power and hard power in social change</u>, by Rt Hon Alan Milburn, MP[1], the former British Secretary of State for Health, at the World Social Marketing Conference in Brighton [in 2008]. This was, for me, the highlight of the meeting: a politician who clearly understood and spoke knowledgeably about social marketing and its implications within the broader social change context we are all working in. Rather than comment on what he said, with the permission of the conference organizers who kindly sent me his text, you can read excerpts I selected (and have added emphasis to in some places) on his vision for the potential role of social marketing in the new politics of empowerment, conversation, social capacity building and engagement:

"From its beginnings in government public information campaigns and through its development since the 1970s into a formal discipline, social marketing is today a life-changing movement. Here in the UK the National Social Marketing Centre has become a repository of good practice and real support to those leading a legion of local efforts to reduce teenage pregnancy rates, tackle alcohol abuse and support sustainable living. <u>Led by the Department of Health, the UK Government has recognised the potency of social marketing in bringing about desirable changes in society. Social marketing is at the heart of many government-backed campaigns, supported by substantial resources from the public purse, on issues like drug awareness, road safety and healthy eating.</u>

Until recently, however, much of your work took place under the radar, ignored by politicians and journalists alike. That is changing. Books like Nudge[2] and Yes[3] have hit the best sellers lists. Their contents are devoured by politicians and public policy makers. Their thinking now finds its way into how policy - from pensions to organ donations - is being constructed. Some even argue that the convergence of insights from social marketing, neuroscience and behavioural economics forms the basis for a new paradigm for social change.

So social marketing has become fashionable. You are no longer in the shadows. You are firmly under the spotlight And of course it's always nice to be popular. But before we all get carried away it's important to recognise the limitations as well as the opportunities inherent in what Robert Cialdini calls "the new science of persuasion." Social change is complex. Behavioral change even more so. It is rarely amenable to a simple single solution. Getting people to eat well and smoke less are desirable social outcomes. But they require a mix of policy tools.

So to fully realise its potential as a force for social change it should do so as an adjunct and not an alternative to what the State does. This is where I believe those on the Right of politics are making such a fundamental strategic error. By rejecting the role of the State they have drawn the wrong conclusion from the modern world. To meet today's policy challenges requires a new balance between what I will call soft power and hard power. Improving health, beating crime, regenerating communities cannot happen if society has to choose between either having an active state or having active citizens. It is not either/or that is needed. It is both. **So I will make the case for a politics of change that has at its core the empowerment of individual citizens and their local communities. And I will argue that social marketing's biggest contribution lies not simply in persuading people to change but in helping empower them to do so...**

We can glimpse what that new future could look like. During my time as health secretary I championed an expert patients programme to give people, mostly those with chronic conditions, the tools to better manage their own care. By putting the individual patient in charge of managing their conditions - the food they ate, the exercise they took, the medicine they used - the programme succeeded in reducing physiotherapy visits by 9%, hospital outpatient visits by 10% and accident and emergency visits by 16%. And as we seek to increase the proportion of spending on public health from a miserly 5% across the developed world - by focusing on preventing not just treating illness as I believe we should - the way to do that is not by preaching at people but by empowering them. Giving people, through our unrivalled UK primary care network of pharmacies, GP surgeries and community services, the practical help they need - blood pressure monitors, testing kits, food co-ops - to improve their own health. To do that we need to convert patients from being passive recipients of care in a system that denies them both power and responsibility to being in charge and more responsible for their own health. That will require a new focus on providing accessible information and proper support to empower individual citizens. And, given that different people have different starting points, it will require a national drive to grow social capacity so that across all communities, and not

<u>just some, people can make the choices that are right for them. It is here that</u>
<u>your expertise and insight about what drives change is so sorely needed…</u>

…when it comes to social change it is surely inconceivable that poverty or dis-advantage can be overcome without the State or politics playing its part. Poor people are hardly able to spend their way out of poverty. They need help with education, housing, training, childcare. So it is no more acceptable for today's Conservatives to blame poor people for failing to live healthier lives and urging them to get on their exercise bikes than it was for a previous generation of Conservatives to blame people for being out of work and urging them to get on their push bikes. There is a danger of a new naivete: that the science of persuasion can replace the art of public policy - making when it comes to tackling what are deep and complex social problems. Worse still, that nudging becomes little more than an excuse for rolling back the State and disinvesting in public services.

No one denies, of course, that individual citizens have responsibilities. But so do politicians. The trick is to get the balance right between what each does. Take one example. Over many years campaigns that exhorted people to stop smoking and warnings about the consequences of doing so undoubtedly helped many smokers quit. And in the process these social marketing techniques helped create a permissive climate for political action. In turn that political action, in the form of tax rises on tobacco and smoking cessation on the NHS, helped shift the climate of public opinion still further in favour of tougher action culminating in a legal ban on smoking in public places. The smoking ban could not be nudged into existence: State action had to bring it into existence…

The challenges of the modern world call for the State to play its part but also to know its place. It is only the State that can equalise opportunities throughout life and empower its citizens. Equally only citizens can seize those opportunities and realise their own aspirations to progress. So just as the Right is wrong to reject the State's role, the Left must avoid the trap of countering an argument about less state by making a case for more State. **What is needed is a different sort of State: one that empowers, not controls.**

This I believe is the basis for a new politics which has at its core a modern progressive cause: the empowerment of citizens. That can only happen if we get the right mix of policy instruments. In foreign policy circles the contemporary debate following the West's interventions in Iraq and Afghanistan is about the necessary balance between hard power and soft power. Hard power is expressed through military force and economic sanction; soft power through careful diplomacy and economic or cultural engagement. Some argue a preponderance of one approach to the other, but the lesson of history is surely that a mix of both approaches is necessary. In the Cold War mutual assured nuclear destruction and NATO may have provided deterrence and safety, but the fall of the Berlin Wall owed at least as much to the attractions of a dynamic mixed economy, blue jeans, the Beatles, the Voice of America and the BBC World Service.

Similarly I think the concepts of soft and hard power can be used to delineate the various instruments that are needed to bring about desirable behaviour and social change in a complex modern society. By "hard power" I mean the use of laws, regulations and formal incentives to reinforce social norms. By "soft power," I mean the array of community engagement and social marketing tools that you are so versed in. In my view getting the right balance between soft and hard power is the key to unlocking social progress and opening the way to a modern relationship between state and citizen.

I welcome the fact that the National Social Marketing Centre is taking a leading role in this debate through its own reviews and the growing recognition within the social marketing profession of the need to achieve the right balance. The soft power/hard power distinction finds an echo in the contrast the Centre draws between "strategic social marketing" (that is upstream work using your insight and evidence base to influence public policy making) and "operational social marketing" (that is downstream work implementing social marketing techniques on the ground). It is when the two are allied that most progress is made. Conversely as a recent research report into the effectiveness of UK government funded social marketing campaigns highlights, a lack of integration between a campaign and broader governmental strategies can undermine its potential impact on positive behavioural change.

This suggests to me that public policy makers have not as yet fully appreciated the benefits that social marketing and behavioural change techniques can bring to bear on making social change happen. One way of correcting this understanding deficit would be to make training in social marketing and behavioural change part of the package that public officials in health, education, estates management and local government automatically receive. So that those officials engaged in community regeneration, for example, would have their focus as much on hearts and minds as bricks and mortar…

In 1945 the new idea was for power to be vested in the central state and its policy expression was nationalisation. In 1979 the new idea was for power to be vested in the free market and its policy expression was privatisation. In 1997 the new idea was for power to be vested in reformed institutions and its policy expression was modernisation. Now **the new idea is to vest power in the citizen and the community and to make its policy expression empowerment.** This is the new political territory. Neither the Right nor the Left have in truth, yet fully come to terms with it. Whoever does so first I believe will win both ideologically and electorally. I hope you will play a leading role in making it happen.
[Ed Note: Now to find the US politician who can deliver as eloquent an argument.]

Notes

1. http://en.wikipedia.org/wiki/Alan_Milburn
2. Thaler, R.H, Sunstein, C.R. *Nudge: Improving Decisions About Health, Wealth, and Happiness.* Caravan Books: caravanbooks.org, 2008.
3. Goldstein, N.J., Martin, S.J., Cialdini, R.B. *Yes!: 50 Scientifically Proven Ways to Be Persuasive.* New York: Simon and Schuster, 2008.

Social Marketing and Democracy

With the presidential nomination process claiming most of the news holes in the US, the authors of *Greater Good: How Good Marketing Makes for Better Democracy*[1] are interviewed at the Harvard Business School Working Knowledge[2] site. Here are some salient excerpts for social marketers and government officials.

...what's needed in politics is not less marketing but better marketing. The two major parties should focus on learning current and emerging citizen needs, developing policy and program solutions, informing interested citizens about themselves, and making themselves easily accessible. They should embrace reforms, such as lifelong voter registration, that remove barriers to participation. Politicians need to view citizens not as occasional voters, donors, and taxpayers but as their customers.

Q: In the United States it seems the public has a very low opinion of the federal government. Can government market itself more effectively to its constituents and customers?

A: *The federal government and local governments can market themselves more effectively to constituents. First of all, they have to view their organization from a customer viewpoint and ask: Who are our customer groups? How are we going to add value to those customers?*

Federal agencies that provide services to citizens can institute service improvements and metrics modeled after those in the private sector. They can call on social marketers to aid in communicating with customers and creating attractive exchanges that will achieve desired customer behavior.

And this closing thought - . . . *what is needed is an international institute funded by multiple countries, representing different models of democracy, to create full demand for democracy around the world.*

Sometimes I hear people wonder aloud: is social marketing losing its relevance? Articles like this lead me to believe we are just finding it.

Notes

1. Quelch, J.A., Jocz, K.E. *Greater Good: How Good Marketing Makes for Better Democracy.* Boston, MA: Harvard Business School Publishing, 2007.
2. http://hbswk.hbs.edu/item/5774.html

The Change We Need: New Ways of Thinking about Social Issues

One definition of insanity[1] is *doing the same thing, over and over again, but expecting different results.* As we enter another era of change, will we continue thinking about and trying to solve social and public health issues using the same paradigms and tools, or will rediscovering social innovation[2] lead to original and improved solutions?

Coping with the many challenges confronting our country and world requires, just like with individuals under stress, the development of new ways of coping with them. Economic and policy initiatives are only partial solutions to issues as diverse as safer neighborhoods, childhood obesity and poverty. Education and information campaigns only go so far in reducing the use of tobacco products, increasing the use of preventive health services and engaging parents in their children's education. Laws and regulations improve the safety of our food supply, reduce environmental pollutants and protect against unintentional injuries involving all types of consumer products – yet they too are only partial solutions.

The use of marketing principles and practices in the private sector has been demonstrated to be among the most important sources of success in solving the core business problem of achieving organizational success (generating profits) through satisfying consumer wants and needs. Marketing goes beyond advertising and sales. When applied as intended, it becomes **a systematic way for management to structure its relationships with consumers and stakeholders from the products and experiences it offers, the structure of the incentives and costs associated with them, and their accessibility to how they are promoted in the marketplace with an ever expanding palette of communication tools.** This same marketing management approach should be adopted in the analysis, planning, implementation and sustainability of programs aimed at social problems.

Social marketing, the application of the marketing discipline to social issues and causes, provides a framework for developing innovative solutions to social problems that have long perplexed and frustrated us (See: *Making Change Happen: The Marketing Approach*). It has emerged from business marketing practice as **a social change tool uniquely suited to achieve social profits by designing** integrated programs that meet individual needs for moving out of poverty, enabling health, improving social conditions and having a safe and clean environment. Marketing principles are embedded in such success stories as the Grameen Bank enabling poor people to earn a sustainable income in developing countries, reducing teenage smoking rates in the truth® campaign, improving children's food choices and what they eat in schools through Team Nutrition and reducing childhood deaths from malaria though the distribution of insecticide-treated mosquito nets in endemic countries. Indeed, when we examine some of the more well-known and successful public health programs over the past three decades, the principles of social marketing are being applied by the US Agency for International Development, the Centers for Disease Control and Prevention, the National Institutes of Health and the Office of National Drug Control Policy among others.

Individuals in our society do not live in just a consumer or economic marketplace where monetary concerns and self-interest reign supreme and rational decision-making is believed to be the norm. People's everyday lives include exposure to all types of ideas and behaviors, whether through their family and friends or through television and the internet. **The recognition that these marketplaces of ideas and behaviors also exist, and are subject to forces such as proximity and access, incentives and costs, role models and social norms, health and digital literacy and the quality of their communications environment illuminates how programs that focus on only economic levers, or education, or laws and their enforcement fail to achieve all the social good that is intended.** Similarly, understanding that individual and social change are products of a marketplace of ideas and behaviors that are, in turn, constantly being shaped by the activities of public, private and nonprofit sector actors means that all of these actors must become part of sustainable, long-term solutions and not merely bit players (or partners) in short-term campaigns – if they are engaged at all.

To move society forward in developing new ways of addressing old problems, I suggest that policy-makers in all three sectors of society that agree on areas of common concern – recognizing that there are many different concerns that involve often different sets of actors – begin to adopt these premises of a social marketing perspective in their work.

There must be **a set of integrated activities that analyze, design for, implement and evaluate programs** that specifically address (1) products, services
and behaviors that will improve individual and social well-being; (2) realign
incentives and costs to facilitate behaviors for the individual and social good;
(3) create opportunities and improve access to beneficial products, services
and places that encourage and support behavior change; and (4) employ state-
of-the-science communication strategies and tools to promote and support
positive change at all levels of society - individuals, families and other social
networks, organizations and communities.

Programs should be audience-centric; that is, based on understanding the
people to be served by the program, having insights into how they perceive the
problem and possible solutions in the context of their everyday lives, and engaging them to be co-creators and eventual owners of relevant solutions.

Audience engagement, from who is sitting at the policy table to who is sitting
across from a teacher, **is both a core value and outcome for success.** It becomes
part of a common framework for understanding and implementing programs
with population-wide benefits.

And finally, I look forward to a time when marketing becomes a lingua franca[3]
for all agencies involved in social change activities rather than the current bal-
kanization of efforts by agencies that are fueled by their own unique frameworks
and theories for how problems exist and how they should be solved. Bringing
together public, private and nonprofit (NGO) sectors face this challenge; so too
do multi-sector approaches that attempt to bring together agriculture, education, environment, healthcare, health promotion, transportation, housing, law
enforcement and other actors. Until people and agencies share common frameworks for understanding and communicating with each other, do not expect
much beyond blind men describing an elephant[4].

I know that in some quarters marketing as practiced in the commercial sector is
sharply criticized. Yet **marketing as it can be thought about and practiced for
social change may be one way to have the types of multiple sector, integrated
collaborations that are needed to solve many of the wicked social problems
that have been intractable for too long for so many.**

[Ed Note: This post was subsequently published as - Lefebvre, R.C. The change we need: New ways of thinking about social issues. *Social Marketing Quarterly*, 2009;15:142-144.]

Notes
1. http://en.wikiquote.org/wiki/Rita_Mae_Brown
2. http://www.ssireview.org/articles/entry/rediscovering_social_innovation/
3. http://en.wikipedia.org/wiki/Lingua_franca
4. http://en.wikipedia.org/wiki/Blind_Men_and_an_Elephant